Harald Bergbauer | Yeonho Lee [eds.]

Cooperation in Asia and Disintegration in Europe?

Proceedings of a German-Korean Academic Dialogue

 **Nomos**

The publication of this volume has been made possible by the generous support of the Bavarian School of Public Policy, Munich.

The Deutsche Nationalbibliothek lists this publication in the Deutsche Nationalbibliografie; detailed bibliographic data are available on the Internet at http://dnb.d-nb.de

ISBN   978-3-8487-2021-7 (Print)
         978-3-8452-6100-3 (ePDF)

British Library Cataloguing-in-Publication Data
A catalogue record for this book is available from the British Library.

ISBN   978-3-8487-2021-7 (Print)
         978-3-8452-6100-3 (ePDF)

Library of Congress Cataloging-in-Publication Data
Bergbauer, Harald / Lee, Yeonho
Cooperation in Asia and Disintegration in Europe?
Harald Bergbauer / Yeonho Lee (eds.)
169 p.
Includes bibliographic references.

ISBN   978-3-8487-2021-7 (Print)
         978-3-8452-6100-3 (ePDF)

1. Edition 2016
© Nomos Verlagsgesellschaft, Baden-Baden, Germany 2016. Printed and bound in Germany.

Preface

On July 5-6, 2014 the *Munich School of Policital Science* and the *Institute of East and West Studies* of Yonsei University, Seoul, organized their fourth international conference on political and economic issues (the first one took place in Seoul in 2010, the second one in Munich in 2011, and the third one again 2012 in Seoul). The topic of the fourth conference was *Efforts of Integration in Asia and Fears of Disintegration in Europe,* the meeting place was in the idyllic area of Wildbad Kreuth, one of the conference centers of the Hanns Seidel Foundation in the Bavarian Alps.

The conference spanned a wide range of topics, dealing first with economic and ecological developments in Korea, second with Korea's relations to Russia, and third with the case of Cambodia as a possible exemplar of reunification for Korea. The last and most comprehensive section was dedicated to political and economic analyses of power shifts in Europe in the wake of the current financial crisis. The presentations were made by German and Korean scientists; a number of students and university teachers participated in the meeting and enriched the discussions with various questions and comments.

The articles collected in this volume have their origin in this meeting. The editors gave the authors time to elaborate on their articles until the beginning of 2015. The reference to studies published in 2015 in some of the articles shows that some of them have been reviewed and updated until the middle of 2015.

The editors want to express their gratitude for the support of the conference on the German side to the *Bavarian School of Public Policy*, its alumni association, and the *Hanns Seidel Foundation*, and on the Korean side to the *Institute of East and West Studies* of Yonsei University and to *BMW Korea*. We hope that the reading of the volume will be in the same way instructive and inspiring as the conference was.

Munich and Seoul 2015   Harald Bergbauer
                                                                Yeonho Lee

Table of Contents

Introduction

In 1993, a few years after the collapse of communism the American author Francis Fukuyama published a book on *The End of History and the Last Man*. The book became a worldwide bestseller. The main thesis was that history in terms of its political order and institutions is coming to an end because democracy in connection with capitalism proved superior and, lastly, victorious compared to socialism; it will be followed, sooner or later, by all other political and economic regimes. Today, more than 25 years after the break-up of the Soviet Union and its satellite states, skepticism prevails with respect to democracy's and capitalism's superiority. Many countries are still struggling with the aftermath of the economic crisis of 2008, the United States does not seem to be the world's uncontested leading power anymore, and Europe is obviously caught in a financial quagmire due to the construction of the European Monetary Union which clearly overstrains the economic power of some of EU's member states. Other regions of the world are in turmoil, too. The developments of the Arab Spring in the past years dashed many dreams and hopes, and the competition from illiberal capitalist countries such as China is challenging the whole global economic order set up in the last decades.

Against this background the articles of the present volume pick up some current topics that are of interest for scientists, politicians and ordinary people alike. The present book tackles international events and developments in Europe and East Asia. Scientists from Germany and Korea analyse and describe important issues their societies are faced with. In dealing with a certain topic the authors explain a particular issue and communicate its special feature as well as possible future perspectives to their dialog partners. The underlying intention is to make the reader acquainted with the issue itself and to deliver prospective solution models. Given the wide range of topics which focus both on different continents and issues, the participants exchanged relevant information on distant and important areas. The topics are in particular focusing on four different areas.

I. Under the heading *Political and Economic Developments in Korea* the first article deals with *Environmental Politics in Korea: Ecologism vs. Tokun-state*. Taedong Lee emphasizes the contrast between a civil society-based ecological policy and a government-centered Tokun state policy.

The latter pursues, among others, huge engineering construction projects, harming thereby nature and undermining citizen participation. The essay highlights various aspects of the traditional and modern understanding of the state. The second article extends the perspective by focusing on *The North Korean Economy within the Gravity of South Korea and China*. Doowon Lee maintains that after the early 1990s North Korea, due to self-inflicted isolation, has lost most of its trading partners, except China and, partially, South Korea. Using the gravity model of trade he states that North Korea's trade volume in 2012 was $ 16 billion, whereas in 2014 it shrank to $ 6 billion. The inter-Korean trade volume also fell from $ 43 billion in 2012 to $ 2 billion in 2014. The gap between the actual and the potential trade volume is huge and – most importantly – could be diminished if politically intended. It's up to politics to pave the way to improve the living conditions especially in North Korea.

II. Part two deals with *South Korea's Relations to Russia*. Sangtu Ko analyzes the *Nationalism in Russian Foreign Policy*. Starting with theoretical considerations of whether domestic policies determine international politics, or vice versa, the author maintains that nationalism gained great significance in Russian society with increasing repercussions in international relations, West and East. The cases of Georgia and Ukraine (so far) serve as two examples to illustrate Russia's nationalism and its international implications. In the subsequent article Werner Gumpel reports about *Russia as Provider of Energetic Resources for Europe and Korea: Problems and Approaches to Solutions*. Russia is one of the biggest energy exporters of the world, providing natural gas and crude oil, on which both Europe (and here most strongly Germany) and - North and South - Korea depend. Russia consciously utilizes this important position.

III. The topic of reunification is dealt with under the heading *Cambodia as an Exemplar of Reunification for Korea?* (Experiences of German re-unification in the 1990s have been discussed in previous years.) Gottfried-Karl Kindermann analyzes *The Role of International Diplomacy (especially the UN) in the Course of the Peaceful Re-Unification of Cambodia*. He distinguishes three kinds of reunifying divided countries: reunification by conquest (Vietnam), by the vigor of its own population (Germany), and by the assistance of the UN (Cambodia). The article shows how governments of antagonistic systems were put under a temporary trusteeship of the UN in order to set up a united government.

IV. The last and most comprehensive part focuses on *Power Shifts in Europe in the Wake of the Current Financial Crisis* and offers both political and economic analyses. Harald Bergbauer tackles the *Political Power Shifts in Europe as a Result of the Economic and Financial Crisis in Europe*. He maintains that in the wake of the financial crisis in Europe the common currency didn't contribute to strengthen the relations or even to help unite the member states of the European Union, but he assumes that it rather loosened and deteriorated their relations. Due to weak economic performances especially in France (but also in other Southern European states) in recent years it seems that the former Franco-German axis is (partly) being replaced by a new and strong relationship between Germany and Poland. A process of restructuring of the EU is underway. Dealing with *The Political and Economic Effects of the Eastward Expansion of the European Union for Germany*, Ralf Goellner picks up this argument and investigates the relationship of Germany and the Central East European countries in detail. He analyzes first the political effects on Germany as a result of the first two rounds of the Eastern European enlargement in 2004 and 2007, and outlines, second, the enlargement effects on the German economy and its labor market. Germany turns out not only as the biggest exporter to Eastern Europe, but as the most important importer of Eastern European goods, too.

The last two articles of the present volume tackle the financial crisis from a purely economic point of view. Rigmar Osterkamp, talking about *Rescuing the Euro – Consequences for the Future of the Euro and of Europe*, describes the (positive and negative) effects of the Euro rescue measures and speculates about possible future rescue operations and their effect for the Euro and the project of the European Union. He postulates that a bankruptcy procedure for governments and banks be instituted, and that under certain conditions exit strategies for member states be provided for. The concluding article is on *The International Financial Crisis and its Effects on the World Economy*. According to its authors, Heinz Steinmueller and Jona van Laak, Europe is facing two crises: the first one has its cause in the housing-bubble in the USA, the second one consists in the weakness of the Euro itself. Both could have been avoided or at least be cured if basic rules and principles of free-market economics had not been disobeyed, like, for example, transparency, non-destructive competition, a certain degree of regulation, etc. And only by restoring these (and other) fundamental rules of free-market economics Europe – and other parts of the world – will overcome the current crisis and (hopefully) resist future financial dangers.

The topic of the present publication is *Cooperation in Asia and Disintegration in Europe*. The introduction of the common currency in now 19 member states of the European Union since 1999 was a huge step in European integration. On the one hand, the single currency was one of Europe's major successes: almost 350 million people in Europe use the Euro as their currency and enjoy its benefits; the Euro is the daily used symbol of an integrated Europe. But the Euro is, on the other hand, also one of Europe's major dangers: it harmonized very different and heterogeneous national economies and generated thereby various tensions between Europe's nation states. A cleavage between the Northern and Southern European countries became manifest during the last years. The case of Greece is only the most prominent instance, other especially South-European countries could easily be added. The Euro as the main instrument which pursued the aim of binding the European states closer together generated also very opposite effects. A certain disintegration in Europe comes to the fore.

The measure of integration in East Asia is totally different in quantity and quality. Such an ambitious project like the European integration does not exist. There is no attempt to create a supranational entity comparable to the European Union which is based on the will of its members to transfer by law sovereign powers to international organizations. The prevailing model in East Asia consists in a (more or less loose) cooperation of states which participate in various regional organizations and which do not transfer sovereign rights to superordinate entities. Political control, however, over the process of economic globalization is regarded indispensable. Important associations for East Asian countries are, for example, the *Asian Pacific Economic Cooperation* (APEC), the *Association of Southeast Asian Nations* (ASEAN), the *Association of Southeast Nations Plus Three* (ASEAN+3 [plus China, South Korea, Japan]), the *Pacific Economic Cooperation Council* (PECC), or the *Asia Cooperation Dialogue* (ACD). All of these - and other not mentioned - organizations bring together politicians, officials and technocrats, the organizations are platforms for representatives to discuss issues of common interest and to make common decisions. Even if the level of integration in these cases is lower than in the case of Europe, the tensions due to different political interests or economic power are clearly beneath those in Europe. The present volume sheds some light on select examples of - successful or failed - integration and disintegration processes.

I)

Political and Economic Developments in Korea

Environmental Politics in Korea: Ecologism vs. Tokun-state. The Cases of Saemangum and Four Rivers Project

Taedong Lee

Abstract

Experiencing compact economic growth and democratization, environmental politics in Korea is the history of ecologism and Tokun-state (state leading mass development projects) which have been competing and confronting each other. The Saemanguem reclamation project and the Four-Major-Rivers project seem to win a triumph of Tokun-state based on massive capital interests and state authoritative forces over ecologism, which is based on ecology-centered civil society organizations. However, the consequences of Korea Tokun-state's power gaining may lead to harmful impacts on the ecosystem, the distribution of financial resources and the democratic process of policy decision-making. This study aims to conceptualize ecologism and Tokun-state, considering actors, values, and strategies through the case study of the Saemanguem project and the Four-Major-Rivers project.

1. Introduction

How do we understand and explain environmental politics in Korea? Environmental politics refers to who, with which value, and how people make decisions on the distribution and conservation of the environment as a common resource. In this regard, studies on environmental politics in Korea aim to understand and explain cooperation and competition between various actors, values and strategies over resources, land, and environment in Korea.

Through the history of rapid modernization, the Korean environment and eco-system have been regarded as resources for economic development and were overused by the state-led massive construction projects. Yet, democratization and the rise of civil society also show that there are critical groups, opposing destructive development projects of the state (and local) government and construction companies. The confrontation over large-scale state development projects illustrates the competition between ecologism and Tokun-state.

This study aims to explain Korean environmental politics by looking at two competing groups in large-scale infrastructure projects. First I describe the concepts of Tokun-state and ecologism considering actors, views on time and nature, the sources of power, strategies, and problems. Then I analyze the two major environment-development projects by examining how Tokun-state and ecologism interpret these projects. The last section concludes with implications of the research.

2. Tokun-state vs. Ecologism

Tokun-state (土建國家) refers to a state that leads large-scale construction projects for the national and local economic development using fiscal policy. After the Great Depression in the US and the after-war period in Japan, government utilized state finance to infrastructure building in the name of revitalizing economic growth (Kenichi 2009). Of course, government-led infrastructure construction projects such as the New Deal policy may be a good solution to ensure economic growth and help the employment rate increase under the condition of underdevelopment and economic recess. Infrastructures are needed for most of the economic activities; massive infrastructure construction projects may be losses rather than gains. In particular, gains from the construction may only go to few and particular groups of people whereas losses are a burden for the ecosystem and the public.

One of the characteristics of Tokun-state can be found in the ratio of the construction industry to GDP. Due to a series of state-led massive construction projects, Korean added value of construction business over GDP was 8.8% from 1995-2006. It was ranked top in the OECD countries and higher than that of Japan (7.36%). Investment on the construction project of the same period is 1.65 times higher (19.22%) than the average of the OECD countries (11.67%) (Yim 2010). This statistics partly shows that reliance on the construction industry is relatively high in Korea.

Table 1 compares ecologism and Tokun-state in the respects of actors, view on the nature and time, power, and strategies. The actors of Tokunism are the state government and politicians. In addition, the engineering and construction industry that benefit from massive construction projects are also major actors. The power source of the state government is a monopolized authority; the power source of the industry comes from the capital and the organizations. These actors tend to have cozy relations in getting 'turn-key' construction contracts in the developmental project. A turn-key contract refers to one company that designs, constructs and tests the complex facility for a client. While it would be sufficient that one company turns over ready-to-use condition facilities to the buyer, it also has been criticized in terms of fairness and transparency (Kim M김명식 2013).

These three actors view nature as an object to be overcome and utilized. In the industrialization period, the state apparatus and industries have extracted resources from nature in the name of economic development, which leads to massive destruction and quality degradation (Hwang and Park 2010). If there is untouched nature, it becomes a construction site for development and economic growth (서왕진 (Seo 2010)).

They tend to view time in a short-term perspective. Political leaders are likely to want to present their performance visually within their term; the construction industry seeks to increase net benefits within short or mid-term. To achieve the short-term goal, Tokun-state pushes the timeline and the due as well as it pours available resources. The gap between short-term political and economic interests and their long-term impacts on nature and society tend to become wider.

Despite the benefits that Tokunism provides for infrastructure, it also begets serious problems. First, fiscal policies for constructing infrastructure increase the debt of national, local and public companies. Mostly due to the massive construction projects, Korean national debt increased from 30 billion (USD) in 2008 to 50 billion in 2013 (임석민 (Lim 2010)). Second, Tokun-state is keen to spend a substantial amount of money on a large-scale infrastructure construction project such as the Four-Major-Rivers project (about 2 billion USD within a short term (three years). This quick money spending is like to beget corruption and iniquity. The National Audit Bureau reported some corruption and iniquity cases (감사원 2013). Third, quick top-down decision making cannot guarantee democratic participation in the decision-making process. Despite the critical ecological impact and substantial financial investment, a deliberative consideration of the impacts and resource allocation is lacking.

Table 1. Comparison between Ecologism and Tokun state

	Ecologism	Tokun-state
Actors	Civil society, NGOs	State; Construction industry
Nature	Conservation	Development objectives
Time	Long-term perspective	Short-term perspective
Power Source	Citizen participation	Public authority; capital
Strategies	Bottom-up, solidarity, critics	Top-down, Speed war
Problems	Limited available resources	Corruption, fiscal debt

Ecologism argues that environmental problems are not only the domain of natural science but also that of social issues that become politicized (황진태 (Hwang and 박배균 (Park 2013)). The primary actor of ecologism is civil society. The term civil society is somewhat ambiguous. More concrete actors of ecologism are environmental organizations that pursue harmony between human needs and the natural carrying capacity. To confront Tokun-state, locally-based civil organizations formed solidarity networks with other organizations and researchers to enhance the awareness of the pertinent environment issues.

Environmental nongovernmental organizations (NGOs) are "strategic organizations whose arsenal includes the formation of coalitions, tactical lobbying and multi-level campaigning" on environmental matters (Botetzagia et al. 2010). Networking is a linkage of small and big environmental NGOs in forming a coalition. The networks of environmental NGOs can be considered as "open, flexible, dynamic, horizontal organizational forms or sets of interconnected nodes—as opposed to hierarchies and market-based exchanges." They "communicate sharing values or goals in a voluntary, reciprocal and horizontal" way (ibid pp. 115-116). These networks seek the power of coalition by disseminating ideas, research, and information, by reducing isolation, and by increasing access, efficiency, visibility, and legitimacy. Thus, the source of power for ecologism comes from citizen participation in organizations and networks of various environmental campaigns.

Ecologism interpreted the same fact (construction project) according to shared norms and cultural bias, setting strategies in line with norms that are contradicting those of Tokun-state (Kim 2003). To them, the environment itself has value to be conserved rather than being a pure objective for development. With the slogan, "Rivers must run", NGOs protested against the Four-Major-Rivers project, approaching development issues with a critical perspective on human intervention in nature. In this regard, the view of ecologism on nature is different to that of Tokun-state. Ecologism views people as a part of nature rather than a resource for human use (Kim 2008). Thus, ecologism seeks a way of life in harmony with nature instead of destroying and degrading nature in the name of economic development.

Above all, ecologism puts an emphasis on the long-term impacts of Tokun state's construction projects in society and the ecosystem. It is mainly because of the meaning of sustainability as a primary value that ecologism pursues. Sustainable development refers to the way of harmonizing the three pillars of economic, societal, and environmental values, considering the future generation's needs as well as those of the current generation. Therefore, the long-term horizon of any development projects is the concern of ecologism.

While many people share the values and viewpoints of ecologism, they often lack human, material and information resources, compared to Tokun-state. First, the lack of civic participation limits the funding source for activities. Compared to relatively abundant funding through tax revenues and industrial sales revenues, actors in ecologism do not have reliable sources of financing except for membership fees. Ecologism is also short of human and information resources to look carefully over the plethora of ongoing and upcoming massive construction projects. Since most information on large-scale development projects is classified, actors having ecologist interests tend to react to already decided projects rather than to prepare alternatives in advance. Tokun state actors may not respond to the criticism from ecologism because they may know the human and material limitation of ecologism.

3. Tokun state and Ecologism in the Saemanguem Project

The Saemanguem project, initiated in 1991, aimed to reclaim the wetland into 283 km^2 (about 40,000 hectares) of land for agriculture and the industry zone by constructing 33.9 km levy in the Jeorabook province. The central government (particularly the Ministry of Agriculture and Forestry and Agriculture), the local government (Jeorabook province), and some residents support the Saemanguem project. They believe that the reclaimed area, which is two-thirds of Seoul's area, can be used for regional development. The completion of the project took 21 years from 1991 to 2011 with a budget of US $2.1 billion (Cho 2007).

Figure 1. the Saemanguem reclamation project (source: Jung, Joohee)

The Tokun-state, based on the firm relationship between the government and the construction industry, reclaims the Saemanguem area. They regard nature and land as a resource for economic development. The Ministry of Agriculture defends the needs of the Saemanguem project to expand the land for agriculture, to secure water resources, and to pursue a balanced development in the Jeorabook province. Politicians (including President Taewoo Rho and Dae Jung Kim) echoed to the claim of economic development in relatively underdeveloped areas to gain more political support. The Jeorabook province also regarded that the Saemanguem project as large-scale civil engineer construction would boost their local economy with the national budget. Within a short-term period, bureaucrats and politicians, having the support of local developers, turned the wetland area into land for human needs and economic benefits (박순열 (Park 2007)).

Table 2. Ecologism and Tokun state in the Saemanguem project

	Ecologism	Tokun state
Actors	Green Korea United, KFEM, Religious groups, regional environmental NGOs, scholars	Ministry of Agriculture; Jeorabook Province, construction industry, regional development civil organization, engineering scholars
Nature	Peace and life, conservation of wetland	Reclaiming wetland into agriculture land; comprehensive development for international trade
Time	Future generation	Election (5 years)-term; construction project duration
Power Source	Local knowledge; citizen and media support	Public authority; capital
Strategies	Issue framing; Sambo-Il-bae campaign; Legal cases	Ignoring voices; rapid construction
Problems	Limited available resources	Mismatch between goal and practice

However, environmental NGOs including the Korea Federation of Environmental Movement and Green Korea United opposed the Saemanguem project, arguing that levy construction and the reclamation of wetland could lead to water quality degradation and wetland habitat destruction (Kim 2012). In 1996, Green Korea United and Korean Federation for Environmental Movement claimed that the wetland in the Saemanguem area has ecological values for migratory birds and the marine ecosystem. One of the primary reasons that environmental NGOs opposed the Saemanguem project was the water quality degradation in the Shihwa reclaimed project. The Shihwa project was similar to Saemanguem, which brought ecological concerns on large-scale reclamation projects. Along with other 39 national and regional NGOs, civil organizations formed the "Civil Committee to Abolish Saemanguem Reclamation Project" in 1998 to raise questions about the Saemanguem project (남상민 (Nam 2005)).

One of the primary mottoes of ecologism is "the wetland is alive." This statement presents the ecologism's viewpoint on nature. The wetland itself has various ecological values. Reclaiming wetland into agriculture land is only beneficial to the human being. To make a counter-argument, ecological groups highlight the social and environmental aspects of development, which discuss the economic benefits of the construction dominantly.

Ecologist groups adopted a variety of campaigns such as Sambo-ilbae (three steps and one bow) from the Saemanguem area to Seoul and other major cities to increase the awareness of the destruction of large wetland areas and the ecosystem. Arguments from two confronting groups went to the court but sunk cost arguments allowed Tokun-state to reclaim the Saemanguem area. (Kim 2008). Due to the limitation of the human and financial resources, ecologism could not engage in the Saemanguem project in the early stage. Thus, the construction project was already on the way, which increased so-called sunk cost.

As seen in the above theory section, the Saemanguem case shows the conflicts and confrontation between Tokun-state and ecologism over large-scale development. The Saemanguem reclamation project illustrates the conflicts with ecologism and Tokun-state where distinguishable perspective and power sources are not likely to settle down quickly. It also shows that Tokun-state having more resources compared to ecologist groups is likely to pursue its goal for economic development (Kim 2003).

4. Four major rivers project

The four major rivers in Korea refer to Han River, Guem River, Yongsan River and Nakdong River. The stated goals of the Four Major Rivers Restoration Project are to solve water scarcity, enhance flood controls, and promote water efficiency in these rivers. The beginning of the project came from the problems of the existing watershed management system. Extant management presented the lack of comprehensive management strategies, a weak relation between upstream and downstream, and large city oriented facility construction (한국환경부 2006).

Figure 2. The Four Major Rivers Restoration Location (Source: Ministry of Land, Transport, and Maritime Affairs, Korea)

This project has been controversial due to its ambitious developmental goals covering all major rivers in Korea (김창수 (Kim 2013)). President Myung-bak Lee declared 'Low Carbon Green Growth' as primary national agenda. The Four Rivers Restoration project became part of the Green New Deal, which creates green growth through increasing green jobs and a new water management system. However, some professors, religious leaders, and environmental NGOs insisted that the four rivers projects will destroy the ecological system without social and economic benefits. The Four-Major-Rivers project shows how Tokun-state and ecologism group clash over a large-scale infrastructure construction project.

The Lee regime originally proposed a four rivers channel project in 2007, which faced severe opposition from civil society with 'candle light' demonstrations. The Lee administration changed the name and aim of the project by switching from a channel to river 'restoration'. Having a green image in the name of green growth, the state led a neo-liberal developmental strategy to boost up real estate development and construction industry. As the private construction market faced the risk of bankruptcy, the public (state) provided mass construction engineering projects like the Four Rivers construction. Tokun-state actors made a firm alliance again for this project (이해진 (Lee 2012)).

Regarding the view of nature, there were many construction sites that ignore the existing natural habitats. For example, as part of the four rivers development projects, the government constructed one of the largest scale sport facilities including one sport complex building, ten soccer fields, two baseball fields, ten badminton courts, in Gumi City, Kyounbook province. Next to the construction site, there was a sign for natural habitat protection areas of migratory birds (김명식 2008).

Tokun state in the four rivers project strengthened the alliance using a variety of tactics. The way that Tokun-state implemented the construction projects became much stronger and faster than that of the Saemanguem project. First, the Four-Major-Rivers project spent immense financial and material resources in a rapid manner. Comparing to the Saemanguem project, where 2.1 billion USD were spent in 21 years from 1991 to 2011 (Cho 2007), the River project spent 22 billion USD only for four years (from 2009 to 2012) across nation-wide construction sites.

Second, there lacked efforts to reconcile the different views on the Four-Major-Rivers project, while some efforts sought common ground for various groups in the Saemanguem project (김명식 (Kim 2011). The Saemanguem project formed a collaborative research team of ten experts recommended by environment NGOs, eleven experts recommended by the government, and nine governmental officers to comprehensively investigate the economic and environmental (particularly water quality and ecosystem) impacts of the project (새만금사업환경영향공동조사단 2000). In addition, to solve the continuing conflicts between the two groups, there was legal dispute from the first level court to the supreme court decision. The Four-Major-Rivers project lacked a legal procedure to consider different values and perspectives on the impacts of massive infrastructure developmental projects (Park 2009).

The rapid and no-consensus construction process of the Four-Rivers project brought policy conflicts between Tokun-state and ecologism in each river. In 2010, organic farmers, the Korea Federation of Environmental Movement, and the Goyang Federation of Environmental Movement protested against the small dam construction in Han River construction sites. In the Nakdong River, Busan Green Korea and Busan Federation of Environmental Movement claimed that the four rivers projects in Nakdong river is destroying the ecosystem in the river estuary. In the Yongsan River and the Guem River there emerged policy conflicts between Tokun-state and ecologism (윤태웅 (Yoon and 임승빈 (Lim 2012)). These conflicts faded away after completing small dam constructions in the rivers.

In the perspective of comprehensive water management, the four rivers project failed to meet sustainability and public interests. Lee argues that the four rivers project did not satisfy the seven principles of an integrated water management policy: water quality management, fiscal sustainability, systematic governance, institutional capacity, fair distribution of cost and benefits, alleviation of poverty, preventing disaster (이상헌 (Lee 2010)).

Conclusion

The aims of Tokun-state are national and regional economic development through gigantic engineering construction projects. However, the review has discussed economic, social and environmental impacts, as well as the distribution of the developmental benefits. As Hong (2005) criticized, Tokun-state shows that the "cozy and firm relationship between the construction industry and state apparatus destroy the environment and waste tax revenue" (p. 22). Groups with ecologism have less power to check and balance the power and capital of Tokun-state. Moreover, if Tokun-state would not listen to the voice from ecologism, it is challenging for ecologism groups to get involved in the decision-making process for a massive infrastructure construction project (홍성태 (Hong 2008)).

While it seems an over-simplified dichotomy between Tokun-state and ecologism to explain environmental politics in Korea, we have witnessed a series of conflicts between the two groups' ideas, power and strategies in mass construction development projects. To balance the power of Tokun-state and ecologism, several policies can be suggested. First of all, institutional change to check the cozy relationship between government and business by monitoring potential corruption. In addition, taking responsibility of flawed demand prediction for large scale construction and ensuring the internal reporting should be in place. Furthermore, strengthening participation from civil society and capacity building for NGOs is also requested. A deliberative democracy that considers long-term impacts of large scale infrastructure construction should be prioritized in the decision-making process. A governance system including civic participation for integrated water and land management is imperative.

REFERENCES

Botetzagia, Iosif, Prue Robinson, and Lily Venizelos. 2010. "Accounting for Difficulties faced in Materializing a Transnational ENGO Conservation Network: A Case-Study from the Mediterranean." Global Environmental Politics 10 (1): 115-51.

Cho, Dong-Oh. 2007. "The Evolution and Resolution of Conflicts on Saemangeum Reclamation Project." *Ocean & Coastal Management* 50: 930-44.

Kenichi, Miyamoto. 2009. "토건 국가를 넘어: 대체적 지역 개발과 일본의 경험." *공간과 사회* 31: 126-37.

Kim, Jung Wk. 2008. "Environmental Conflicts and Activism with Industrialization in South Korea." *Clean* 36: 5-6.

Kim, Pan Suk. 2012. "Advocacy Coalitions and Policy Change: The Case of South Korea's Saemangeum Project." *Administration & Society* 44 (6S): 85-103.

Kim, Seoyong. 2003. "Irresolvable Cultural Conflicts and Conservation/Development Arguments: Analysis of Korea's Saemangeum Project." *Policy Sciences* 36: 125-49.

Park, Changkun. 2009. "A Review of the Master Plan for Four Major Rivers Restoration Project." *환경영향평가* 18 (6): 411-7.

감사원, (National Audit Bureau). 2013. *4대강 살리기 사업 설계 시공 일괄입찰 등 주요계약 집행실태 (Audit of Four River Project Planning and Construction Turnkey Companies).* 서울 (Seoul): 감사원 (National Audit Bureau).

김명식 (Kim, Myung-Sik). 2011. "4대강과 숙의민주주의 (Four Rivers and Deliverative Democracy)." *환경철학 (Environmental Philosophy)* 12: 148-78.

김창수 (Kim, Chang-Soo). 2013. "4대강 살리기 사업의 지속가능성 평가 (An Evaluation of the Sustainability of the 4 Major Rivers Restoration Project) " *지방정부 연구 (Korean Journal of Local Government Studies)* 17 (1): 319-42.

남상민 (Nam, Sangmin). 2005. "정책과정에서의 NGO: 정책옹호동맹모형(ACF)과 새만금 사업에서의 NGO 역할

NGO in Policy Process: Advocacy Coalition Framework and NGOs' Roles in the Saemankun Reclamation Project." *한국정책학회보 (Korean Public Policy Review)* 14 (1): 29-53.

박순열 (Park, SoonYawl). 2007. "새만금 개발을 둘러싼 사회적 갈등의 구조와 특징 (Structure and Perculiarities of Social Conflict around Saemanguem Reclamation Project)." *ECO* 11 (1).

새만금사업환경영향공동조사단, (Collaborative Assement Unit of Environmental Impacts of Saemanguem Project). 2000. *결과보고서: 환경영향분야 (Assessment Report: Environmental Impact)*. 서울 (Seoul): 새만금사업환경영향공동조사단 (Collaborative Assement Unit of Environmental Impacts of Saemanguem Project)

서왕진 (Seo, Wang-Jin). 2010. "정치생태학적 관점에서 본 4대강사업 (Political Ecology Discussion on the Four Major River Project)." *민주사회와 정책연구 (Democratic Society and Policy Studies)* 18: 134-58.

윤태웅 (Yoon, Tae-Woong), and Suhng-Bin) 임승빈 (Lim. 2012. "4대강 개발사업의 정책갈등 사례 비교에 관한 연구 A Study of Policy Conflicts on the 4 Major Rivers Refurbishment Project." *한국정책과학학회보 (Review of Korea Policy Science Association)* 16 (3): 29-59.

이상헌 (Lee, Sang-Hun). 2010. "통합적 수자원 관리 원칙에 의한 4대강 사업의 정당성 검토 (Evaluation over the Legitimacy of 4 Major River Project of Korea with the Viewpoint of Principle of Integrated water managment)." *ECO 환경사회학회지* 14 (1): 63-96.

이해진 (Lee, Hae-Jin). 2012. "4대강사업과 지역개발 정치 (The Four-River Project and the Poltics of Regional Development)." *ECO* 16 (2): 51-87.

임석민 (Lim, Seok-Min). 2010. "대규모 국책사업의 실패사례와 그 원인 및 대책 (The Causes and Countermeasures of Large Scale Failed Public Project Cases)." *민주사회와 정책연구 (Democratic Society and Policy Studies)* 18: 100-33.

한국환경부, (Minstiry of Environment). 2006. *물환경관리 기본계획: 4대강 대권역 수질보전 기본계획 (Water Management Basic Plan)*. 과천: 환경부 (Minstiry of Environment).

홍성태 (Hong, Seong-Tae). 2005. *개발공사와 토건국가: 개발공사의 생태민주적 개혁과 생태사회의 전망 (Development Construction and Tokun State)*. 서울 (Seoul): 한울 (Hanul).

―――. 2008. "한반도 대운하의 실체와 문제: 토건국가의 극단화 (Entities and Problems of the Korean Penisular Grand Canal: Making a Construction State Extreme." *민주사회와 정책연구 (Democratic Society and Policy Studies)* 14: 220-43.

황진태 (Hwang, Jin-Tae), and Bae-Gyoon) 박배균 (Park. 2013. "한국의 국가와 자연의 관계에 대한 정치생태학적 연구를 위한 시론 (Seeing the State-nature Relation in South Korea from the Perspective of Political Ecology)." *대한지리학회지 (Korea Geography Association Review)* 48 (3): 348-65.

The North Korean Economy within the Gravitational Area of South Korea and the People's Republic of China

Doowon Lee

Abstract

After the early 1990s, North Korea has lost its trading partners one by one. After the collapse of socialism, North Korea's trade with most socialist countries has disappeared. Also, due to self-induced economic sanctions that are imposed by the USA, the UN, and Japan, the only country that trades de facto with North Korea is China. Also, South Korea still maintains trade relationships with North Korea that are related to the Gaesung Industrial Complex even after the 2010 sinking of a South Korean military vessel by a North Korean submarine. However, North Korea has tried to increase its trade volume recently, and this effort has made North Korea's reliance on trade even more important today than in the past.

This paper tries to estimate the potential trade volume of North Korea with China and South Korea using the gravity model of trade that has been augmented by adding the FTA dummy variable and the TCI variable. When the potential trade volume is estimated between North Korea and China using China's gravity model, it is found that the potential trade volume as of 2012 would be $16 billion when the actual trade volume is $6 billion. It is also found that the potential inter-Korean trade volume as of 2012 would be $43 billion when the actual trade volume is $2 billion. Therefore, we can conclude that North Korea's trade is substantially underperformed compared to its potential. This huge gap between the actual volume and the potential volume implies that North Korea can substantially increase its trading volume with its neighboring countries by improving its relationship with South Korea, Japan, and USA.

1. Introduction

The current status of the North Korean economy can be summarized as stagnant growth, low and unequally distributed income, and international isolation. The first two characteristics have inflicted the North Korean economy since the early-1990s. After the collapse of socialism, the North Korean economy has suffered from negative growth rates during the 1990s. Even though it managed to maintain positive growth rates in the 2000s, the growth rate is still very low and it fluctuates year by year. As a result, the living standard of the average North Korean household has been deteriorated seriously, and the income inequality increased.[1] On top of these two familiar miseries of North Korea, the North Korean economy is currently suffering from international isolation. International isolation of the North Korean economy began from the mid-2000s, and, in many senses, it was a self-induced phenomenon. The North Korean authority has invited sanctions from the United Nations and USA due to its nuclear weapon program from the mid-2000s. Also, due to the conflict with the Japanese government over the issue of Japanese citizens kidnapped by the North Korean agencies in the past, the Japanese government has also banned trade and investment relations with North Korea from the late 2000s. Furthermore, after the sinking of the South Korean military vessel by a North Korean submarine in 2010, the South Korean government has announced the 'May 24, 2010 Measure'. According to this measure, any commercial transaction between South Korea and North Korea has been banned except those that are related to the 'Gaesung Industrial Complex (GIC)'[2]. After a series of economic sanctions imposed by the UN, the USA, Japan, and South Korea, the only trading and investment partner of North Korea today is China and GIC of South Korea.

This paper will first analyze how the external trade relation of North Korea has been evolved so far. Also, using the gravity model of trade, the author will estimate the potential trade volume of North Korea with China and South Korea. The concluding session will summarize main findings of

---

1 One clear indication of a deteriorating living standard is the life expectancy of the North Korean population. According to Lee & Kim (in Korean, 2011), the life expectancy of the average North Korean decreased from 75 years old in 1991 to 67 years old in 2002.

2 Gaesung Industrial Complex (GIC) was established in 2003 and began operation in 2005. It is an industrial complex inside North Korea where South Korean government and firms invested capital and North Korean labors are employed. According to *Chosun Ilbo*, April 1st, 2013, there are 123 South Korea firms at GIC, and they hire approximately 54,000 North Korean labors at the average monthly wage of $134. For more history and implication of GIC, refer to KDI (in Korean, September 2013)

this paper along with some contemporary issues that can affect North Korea's trade relationship with its neighboring countries.

2. The Evolution of the North Korean Trade Structure

By the early 1990s, North Korea had a substantial amount of trade with Russia, Japan, and China. Also, North Korea had maintained trade relations with a diverse number of countries. Even though North Korea did not engage in trade with South Korea due to political conflicts until 1989, North Korea's trade structure in terms of its trading partners was rather normal as of 1990. However, since the radical market economic reform in 1990, the Russian government has demanded North Korea to settle the trade in hard currency, and the trade volume between North Korea and Russia has shrunk since then. On the other hand, since its first transaction in 1989, the inter-Korean trade volume has increased rapidly until 2008. Initially, the total trade volume between South Korea and North Korea was merely $20 million in 1989. However, this number has increased sharply afterward, and it has reached almost $2 billion by 2008. In 2009, the inter-Korean trade volume shrank a little bit due to the outbreak of the global financial crisis in September, 2008. Even though the South Korean economy has rapidly recovered from the global financial crisis, the inter-Korean trade has been sluggish since 2010 due to the 'May 24, 2010 Measure' stated above.

As a result of international isolation stated above, the only meaningful trading partner to North Korea today is China and GIC of South Korea. Therefore, when we exclude South Korea's GIC, China is virtually the only trading partner to North Korea today. This abnormal trade structure is a serious problem both to North Korea and South Korea. From North Korea's point of view, too much dependence on China in terms of export and import can make the North Korean economy very vulnerable to policy change in China. Also, North Korea does not have enough leverage in terms of price negotiation with China. South Korea is also concerned about China's monopoly in North Korea as South Korean firms are losing trade and investment opportunities in North Korea.

Another characteristic we can find in Figure 1 is that North Korea has increased its trade volume and trade ratio since the late 1990s almost continuously. This characteristic is difficult to understand considering the fact that the North Korean economy has suffered from international isolation

Figure 1 North Korea's Trade Partners and Trade/GDP Ratio

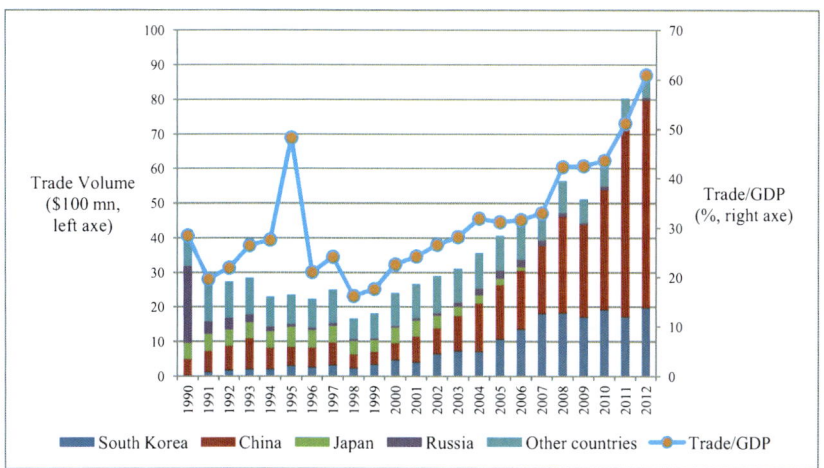

Source: 1990-2010 trade data are from KDI (in Korean, 2010), 2011-2012 trade data are from KOTRA (International trade trend of North Korea 2011, 2012), GDP data are from UN (http://data.un.org)

since the middle of the 2000s. This unique phenomenon is a result of sluggish GDP growth of North Korea and continued efforts of the North Korean government to increase its export. Also, it shows that, unlike the conventional knowledge, the North Korean economy can be influenced by external factors, especially from China.

Let us now examine the trade structure of North Korea by major commodities it exports and imports. Table 1 and Table 2 show major export commodities of North Korea classified by HS 4 digit data in 1990 and 2012. As North Korea traded with various countries in 1990, Table 1 shows the export of North Korea to the world. However, as China is virtually the only country North Korea trades in 2012, Table 2 shows the export of North Korea to China only. As it is shown in Table 1 and 2, North Korea's major export items are mineral products such as zinc and coal and labor intensive products such as apparel. Also, the export structure did not change much between 1990 and 2012. In Table 1 and 2, those export commodities that are shown in both tables are shaded in grey color. Out of 10 major export commodities in 2012, 8 commodities were listed as top 15 export commodities in 1990. It implies that North Korea has failed to improve its comparative advantage during the previous two decades.

Table 1 Top 15 Export Commodities of NK to World (1990)

Commodities	Share (%)
Unwrought zinc	14.3%
Hot-rolled products, iron/steel	8.0%
Coal, briquettes, ovoids etc, made from coal	4.6%
Men or boys suits, jackets, trousers etc not knit	3.5%
Molluscs & aquatic invertebrates nesoi, live etc	2.9%
Women's or girls' overcoats etc, not knit or croch	2.8%
Oil (not crude) from petrol & bitum mineral etc	1.7%
Parts for television, radio and radar apparatus	1.0%
Pig iron & spiegeleisen in pigs, blocks etc	0.7%
Ferroalloys	0.5%
Women's or girls' suits, ensemb etc, not knit etc	0.2%
Electronic integrated circuits & microassembl, pts	0.1%
Motor cars & vehicles for transporting persons	0.1%
Polyethers, expoxides & polyesters, primary forms	0.1%
Track suits, ski-suits & swimwear, not knit etc	0.0%
Total ($ mn)	1,730

Table 2 Top 15 Export Commodities of NK to China (2012)

Commodities	Share (%)
Coal, briquettes, ovoids etc, made from coal	48.5%
Iron ores & concentrates, including roast pyrites	9.9%
Men or boys suits, jackets, trousers etc not knit	3.8%
Molluscs & aquatic invertebrates nesoi, live etc	3.6%
Men's or girls' overcoats etc, not knit or croch	3.5%
Women's or girls' overcoats etc, not knit or croch	3.5%
Pig iron & spiegeleisen in pigs, blocks etc	3.2%
Women's or girls' suits, ensemb etc, not knit etc	2.0%
Unwrought zinc	1.6%
Track suits, ski-suits & swimwear, not knit etc	1.3%
Lead ores and concentrates	1.3%
Precious metal ores and concentrates	1.2%
Magnesite, fused magnesia, d-b magn, m oxide nesoi	1.0%
Electric transform, static converters & induct, pt	0.9%
T-shirts, singlets, tank tops etc, knit or crochet	0.9%
Total ($ mn)	2,502

Similar analysis was made in terms of North Korea's import structure using import data classified by HS 2 digit. Table 3 and 4 show the import structure of North Korea from the world and China respectively in 1990 and 2012. Major import items of North Korea both in 1990 and 2012 are products North Korea cannot produce at home. They are primary products such as oil, heavy products such as machines and steel, and high technology products such as electronical products and vehicles. Also, like the export structure, the North Korean import structure did not change much between 1990 and 2012.

Table 3 Top 15 Import Commodities of NK from World (1990)

Commodities	Share (%)
Wood and article of wood, wood charcoal	9.0%
Iron and Steel	8.4%
Cereals	7.3%
Vehicles other than railway	6.5%
Electrical, electronic equipment	5.6%
Ores, slag and ash	4.1%
Nuclear reactors, boilers, machinery, etc.	4.1%
Mineral fuels, oil, distillation products	3.5%
Cotton	3.5%
Rubber and articles thereof	3.4%
Wool, animal hair, horsehair yarn and fabric thereof	3.0%
Animal, vegetable fats and oils, cleavage products	2.9%
Commodities not specified according to kind	2.9%
Optical, photo, technical, medical, etc apparatus	2.8%
Articles of iron or steel	2.7%
Total ($ mn)	2,440

Table 4 Top 15 Import Commodities of NK from China (2012)

Commodities	Share (%)
Mineral fuels, oil, distillation products	22.2%
Nuclear reactors, boilers, machinery, etc.	8.3%
Electrical, electronic equipment	7.6%
Vehicles other than railway	6.6%
Plastics and articles thereof	3.7%
manmade filaments	3.7%
Cereals	3.6%
Rubber and articles thereof	2.6%
Manmade staple fibres	2.4%
Iron and Steel	2.3%
Animal, vegetable fats and oils, cleavage products	2.1%
Fertilizers	2.0%
Milling products, malt, starches, inulin, wheat glute	1.9%
Articles of apparel, accessories, knit or crochet	1.8%
Articles of iron or steel	1.8%
Total ($ mn)	3,532

From the above analysis, we can conclude that North Korea's trade structure in terms of commodities did not change much during the last two decades. However, North Korea has increased the volume of trade, and it has lost most of its trading partners except China during the same period.

3. Estimating Potential (Normal) Trade Volume of North Korea with China and South Korea

As it is analyzed in the previous section, North Korea's trade pattern today is rather abnormal. Unlike other developing countries, its trade structure in terms of commodities did not change much during the last two decades. Besides, it trades only with China. This abnormal trade pattern, however, will change if North Korea escapes from international isolation and opens up its trade regime. If that happens, North Korea's trade pattern will become normal, and we can estimate the potential trade volume of North Korea with its neighboring countries based on the assumption that North Korea will trade normally with the rest of the world. This session will try to estimate the potential trade volume of North Korea with its two major trading partners, China and South Korea, using the gravity model of trade.

The gravity model of trade can estimate the potential trade volume between two countries based on two countries' GDP, GDP per capita, and distance. This model assumes that two countries' trade volume will be larger as the product of two countries' income is greater. Also, it assumes that two countries' trade volume will be larger as the distance between these two countries is shorter. Therefore, conventional gravity models usually use three explanatory variables to estimate the potential trade volume between two countries. They are product of two countries' GDP, product of two countries' GDP per capita, and distance between the two countries. Besides these three explanatory variables, recent literatures add more variables in order to augment the basic gravity model. These additional variables are variables that can represent the structural difference/similarity between the two countries, and the dummy variable shows whether these two countries are in the same trading block.

One of the early attempts to use the gravity model to estimate potential (natural) trade structure of North Korea is Noland (2000). Noland (2000) used the 1990 trade data of North Korea, and the result is shown in Table 5.

Table 5 Estimating Natural Trade Structure of North Korea by Noland (2000)

	Actual trade share (%)		Natural trade share (%)
China	23	South Korea	35
Japan	21	Japan	30
South Korea	10	China	13
Russia	4	U.S.	7
Rest of world	42	Rest of world	15
Share of North Korea's total trade in GDP	12		71

Source: Recited from Table 7.2 of Noland (2000, p. 262)

As it is shown, the natural (potential) trade structure of North Korea would be substantially different from its actual trade structure. According to his study, South Korea would be the largest trading partner to North Korea followed by Japan, China and USA. Also, trading with these four largest trading partners will dominate North Korea's trade, and North Korea's trade with the rest of the world would be merely 15%. This early study shows that North Korea's trade volume with South Korea and China could increase dramatically if North Korea opened its trading regime.

Estimating North Korea's Potential Trade Volume with China

In order to estimate the potential trade volume between China and North Korea, let us first estimate the gravity model of China's trade with its trading partners. This paper has used the 2012 trade data of China with its 30 largest trading partners. Explanatory variables to estimate the bilateral trade volume between China and these 30 countries are logarism forms of product of GDP between China and each country, the product of GDP per capita between China and each country, the distance between China and each country. In addition to these variables that are used in the basic gravity model, this paper has added two more variables. They are the trade complementary index between China and each country, and a dummy variable which takes the value of '1' if each country has an FTA (free trade agreement) with China. The estimation equation is stated in Equation (1)-1. This equation is similar to the one used by Sohn (2005). In Equation (1)-1, country i implies China, and country j is each of those 30 trading partners.

Equation (1)-1. Gravity Model Equation for China

$$\ln T_{ij} = \alpha + \beta_1 ln[Y_i \cdot Y_j] + \beta_2 ln\left[\left(\frac{Y}{P}\right)_i \cdot \left(\frac{Y}{P}\right)_j\right]$$

$$+ \beta_3 ln D_{ij} + \beta_4 TCI_{ij} + \beta_5 FTA_{ij} + \varepsilon_{ij}$$

Where T_{ij}: Bilateral trade volume between countries i and j
Y_i, Y_j: GDP (current US $ bn) of country i and j
$\left(\frac{Y}{P}\right)_i$, $\left(\frac{Y}{P}\right)_j$: GDP per capita (current US $) of country i and j
D_{ij}: Distance between capitals of countries i and j
TCI_{ij}: Trade complementarities between countries i and j

FTA_{ij}: FTA dummy variable. Input 1 if two countries made FTA, and input 0 otherwise.

The result of this estimation is shown in Table 6.

Table 6 China: Gravity Model Regression

	Estimate	Std. Error	t value	Pr(>|t|)	
(Intercept)	6.01696	2.35306	2.557	0.017299	**
ln $[Y_{CHN} \cdot Y_j]$	0.44607	0.10813	4.125	0.000384	***
ln $[(Y/P)_{CHN} \cdot (Y/P)_j]$	0.11107	0.09889	1.123	0.27246	
ln $D_{CHN\,j}$	-0.58143	0.15971	-3.641	0.0013	***
FTA	0.13731	0.27156	0.506	0.617722	
TCI	1.22786	0.69633	1.763	0.090575	*

Note: Significance codes are 0.01 '***' 0.05 '**' 0.1 '*'.

Residual standard error: 0.5453 on 24 degrees of freedom
Multiple R-squared: 0.5941, Adjusted R-squared: 0.5095
F-statistic: 7.026 on 5 and 24 DF, p-value: 0.0003589

As it is shown in Table 6, all the signs of estimated coefficients are as we have expected. It implies that China trades more with countries that have large GDP, high GDP per capita, short distance, FTA membership with China, and high degree of trade complementarity. However, statistical significance for GDP per capita and FTA membership are relatively small. In particular, the estimated coefficient for FTA is statistically insignificant. It would be because of the fact that China has not signed FTA with many of its trading partners yet.

Using the results of Table 6, let us now estimate the potential trade volume between China and North Korea as of 2012. In order to do that, we can use the estimated coefficients of Table 6 and insert North Korea's data into each explanatory variable. Equation (1)-2 is the equation that uses estimated coefficients of Table 6.

Equation (1)-2. Estimation of China-NK Trade Volume

$$\ln T_{CNK} = 6.01696 + 0.44607 ln[Y_C \cdot Y_{NK}] + 0.11107 ln\left[\left(\frac{Y}{P}\right)_C \cdot \left(\frac{Y}{P}\right)_{NK}\right] +$$

$$(-0.58143)ln\,D_{CNK} + 1.22786 TCI_{CNK} + 0.13731 FTA_{CNK} + \varepsilon_{CNK}$$

Now, let us insert China and North Korea's data into each explanatory variable of Equation (1)-2. These data are shown in Table 7.

Table 7 Variables of North Korea and China

Year: 2012	GDP (Y, bn $)	GDP per capita (Y/P, $)	Distance (D, miles)	TCI	FTA
China	8,358.40	6,069.72	502.85	0.31024	0
North Korea	14.41	583.00			

As a result, we get the potential trade volume between China and North Korea, which is $\widehat{T}_{CNK}^{(2012)} = \$$ 16 billion. This potential volume is much bigger than the actual trade volume between two countries, which is $T_{CNK}^{(2012)} = \$$ 6 billion.

Estimating North Korea's Potential Trade Volume with South Korea

Now, let us use the same methodology in order to estimate the potential trade volume between South Korea and North Korea. The first step to do this is to estimate the gravity equation of South Korea. Equation (2)-1 is the gravity equation we have used for South Korea. The definition and source of explanatory variables are identical with those used in Equation (1)-1. The only difference is that we do not use the TCI variable as the statistical significance for the TCI coefficient turns out to be extremely low. Equation (2)-1. Gravity Model Equation for South Korea

$$\ln T_{ij} = \alpha + \beta_1 ln[Y_i \cdot Y_j] + \beta_2 ln\left[\left(\frac{Y}{P}\right)_i \cdot \left(\frac{Y}{P}\right)_j\right] + \beta_3 ln D_{ij} + \beta_4 FTA_{ij} + \varepsilon_{ij}$$

The regression result of Equation (2)-1 is summarized in Table 8. As it was expected, all the signs of coefficients are as we have expected. Unlike the case of China, the coefficient for FTA has statistical significance at 10%. It implies that South Korea trades more with its FTA partners.

Table 8 South Korea: Gravity Model Regression

	Estimate	Std. Error	t value	Pr(>|t|)	
(Intercept)	10.67924	2.12428	5.027	0.000035	***
ln [$Y_{SK} \cdot Y_j$]	0.31287	0.08184	3.823	0.00078	***
ln [$(Y/P)_{SK} \cdot (Y/P)_j$]	0.04308	0.09547	0.451	0.65569	
ln $D_{SK\,j}$	-0.69801	0.16362	-4.266	0.0002500	***
FTA	-0.4119	0.2134	-1.93	0.06501	*

Note: Significance codes: 0.01 '***' 0.05 '**' 0.1 '*'

Residual standard error: 0.5674 on 25 degrees of freedom

Multiple R-squared: 0.6161, Adjusted R-squared: 0.5547
F-statistic: 10.03 on 4 and 25 DF, p-value: 0.00005519

Using the results in Table 8, we can estimate the potential trade volume between South Korea and North Korea just like we did for China and North Korea. Equation (2)-2 and Table 9 show these procedures. Unlike the case of China, the dummy variable for FTA is '1' as there would be no trade barrier between South Korea and North Korea if South Korea normalizes its economic relationship with North Korea.
Equation (2)-2. Estimation of SK-NK Trade Volume

$$\ln T_{SK\,NK} = 10.67924 + 0.31287 ln[Y_{SK} \cdot Y_{NK}] + 0.04308 ln\left[\left(\frac{Y}{P}\right)_{SK} \cdot \left(\frac{Y}{P}\right)_{NK}\right] +$$

$$(-0.69801) ln\,D_{SK\,NK} + (-0.4119) FTA_{SK\,NK} + \varepsilon_{SK\,NK}$$

Table 9 Variables of South Korea and North Korea

Year: 2012	GDP (Y, bn $)	GDP per capita (Y/P, $)	Distance (D, miles)	FTA
South Korea	1,130	23052	121.36	1
North Korea	14.41	583.00		

As a result, the potential trade volume between South Korea and North Korea as of 2012 would be $\widehat{T}_{SK\,NK}^{(2012)}$ = $ 43 billion when the actual trade volume is merely $T_{SK\,NK}^{(2012)}$ = $ 1.97 billion. It implies that the inter-Korean trade volume would be 20 times larger if North Korea becomes a normal country.

Let us now compare the main result of this paper with the results of previous literatures that have used a similar methodology to this paper. Table 10 summarizes the main results of existing literatures.

Table 10 Summary of Main Results in Existing Literature

	Base Year	Explanatory Variables	Actual Trade Volume ($ mn)	Estimated Trade Volume ($ mn) (Gap between the actual and the estimate)
Lee, Y.S. (1995)	1990	GDP, GNP per capita, Distance	13	2,200 (169 times)
Sohn (2005)	1995	GDP, GDP per capita, Distance, TCI APEC (Dummy)	287	4,303.9 (15 times)
Lee, DW (2011)	2008	GDP, Distance, RTA (Dummy) TL index	1,820	10,230 ~ 15,126 (5.6 ~ 8.3 times)
This Study	2012	GDP GDP per capita Distance TCI FTA (Dummy)	1,970	43,196 (22 times)

Table 10 shows interesting evolution of research findings over time. For example, Lee (1995) concluded that the inter-Korean actual trade volume was abnormally low compared to the potential trade volume as of 1990 due to many political restrictions imposed on inter-Korean trade. However, the gap between the actual trade volume and the potential trade volume has been narrowed in the following studies as South Korea has gradually increased its economic cooperation with North Korea. In this study, however, this gap is widened again reflecting the fact that the inter-Korean economic relationship has experienced a certain setback after the sinking of the South Korean military vessel in 2010 by a North Korean submarine.

4. Concluding Remarks

It is a well-known fact that North Korea is one of the most isolated countries in the world. In particular, after the early 1990s, North Korea has lost its trading partners one by one. After the collapse of socialism, North Korea's trade with most socialist countries has disappeared. Also, due to economic sanctions imposed by the USA and Japan in the 2000s, the only countries that trade substantially with North Korea are China and South Korea. Even though North Korea has lost most of its trading partners,

North Korea has tried to increase its trade volume recently, especially with China. This effort coupled with stagnant GDP growth has made North Korea's reliance on trade even more important today than in the past. When trade structures are examined, however, North Korea's export and import trade structures in terms of commodities did not change much during the last two decades.

Observing these changes in North Korea's trade volume and structure, this paper tries to estimate the potential trade volume of North Korea with China and South Korea using the gravity model of trade. The conventional gravity model usually uses three explanatory variables to estimate the potential trade volume between two countries. They are product of the GDP of two countries, the product of GDP per capita of two countries, and the distance between two countries. This paper has augmented this conventional gravity model by adding the FTA dummy variable and TCI variable. When the potential trade volume is estimated between North Korea and China using China's gravity model, it is found that the potential trade volume as of 2012 would be $16 billion when the actual trade volume is $6 billion. Also, when a similar methodology is applied to North Korea and South Korea, it is found that the potential trade volume as of 2012 would be $ 43 billion when the actual trade volume is $2 billion. Therefore, we can conclude that North Korea's trade is substantially underperformed compared to its potential.

There can be several factors that can change the current situation. First, if the South Korean government softens its stance with North Korea and removes the trade restrictions it has imposed since 2010, it is very likely that the inter-Korean trade volume would increase rapidly. Second, if North Korea resolves the current conflict with Japan and normalizes its relationship with Japan, North Korea can receive a substantial amount of money in compensation for the suffering during the Japanese colonial era. This compensation fund can be as large as $ 8.5 billion according to Zhang (in Korean, 2008, p. 325). This money can increase North Korea's trade and investment volume rapidly in the short term. More than anything else, the biggest change can come from North Korea's own decision to give up its nuclear weapon program and improve its relationship with the rest of the world. This decision will not only increase North Korea's trade volume with the existing trading partners such as China and South Korea but also increase the trade volume with the other major economies such as USA, EU, and Japan.

References

English References

Frankel, Jeffrey A. and Shang-Jin Wei, "Is a Yen Bloc Emerging?" *Joint U.S.-Korean Academic Studies* 5: 145-175, Korea Economic Institute of America, 1995.

Lee, Doowon, "Estimating the Potential size of Inter-Korean Economic Cooperation", *Joint U.S. -Korea Academic Studies,* Vol. 21, pp. 149-163 (Washington DC: Korea Economic Institute of America, Jan. 2011).

Noland, Marcus, *Avoiding the Apocalypse: the Future of the Two Koreas*, Institute for International Economics, Washington, DC, 2000.

Sohn, Chan-Hyun, "Does the Gravity Model Explain South Korea's Trade Flows?", *The Japanese Economic Review*, Vol. 56, No. 4, pp: 417-430 (December 2005).

Korean References

이석&김두얼, '남북한 장기 경제추세 비교와 대북정책에의 시사점', KDI 정책연구시리즈 10호, 2011.

장형수, "북한개발지원을 위한 국제협력방안: 재원조달방안을 중심으로", 『통일정책연구』, 제17권, 제1호, 2008, pp. 315-338.

KDI 북한경제리뷰 (KDI Review of the North Korean Economy), 2013년 9월. 개성공단.

KDI, 『1990~2008년 북한무역통계의 분석과 재구성』, 2010년 12월.

II)

South Korea's Relationships to Russia

The Rise of Nationalism in Russian Foreign Policy

Sangtu Ko

Introduction

While witnessing Russian President Vladimir Putin's approach to dealing with the recent Ukrainian crisis, both the United States and the European Union expressed concerns that the old Cold War was coming back. The Russian behavior under Putin demonstrates a shift from its traditional approach. The relationship between Russia and the West, as well as its propensity to deteriorate, can be explained by the power shift as Russia has become an emerging power while the unipolar system of the United States has eroded. This change in the power relations seems to have affected Russia's foreign policy.

In addition to the long-term deterioration, Russia's position toward the West has fluctuated, with its foreign policy oscillating between a cooperative and an assertive attitude. The pro-Western position of the Yeltsin administration became more assertive in 1994 after the West had intervened in the former Yugoslavia and NATO pushed forward with an eastward expansion. In response, Yeltsin warned of the danger of a "cold peace." However, Russia was forced to soften its position in 1998 when it declared an IMF moratorium. Russia desperately needed Western help to overcome its economic crisis. The cooperative conduct continued even after Putin came into office with his slogan "Great Power Russia." The September 11 attacks gave Putin the opportunity to offer his assistance in the US war against global terrorism. However, the protracted stationing of American troops in Central Asia soon generated discontent among Russian officials. The Russia–Georgian War subsequently ruptured Russian foreign policy and further culminated in the Ukrainian War.

What are drivers behind this dynamic fluctuation? The external factor (i.e. the power shifts) seems to explain it to a certain extent, yet the structural change of power relations between the United States and Russia is more appropriate for accounting for developments over time. Explaining the fluctuations requires considering internal factors as well. Russia is seen as a paradigm example where domestic social factors and international system factors have intertwining effects on foreign policy making. This paper focuses on Russian nationalism to account for the impulse to be assertive toward the West.

Although international relations theory seeks to explain the state interactions, theories of foreign policy are interested in the behaviors of individual states. Each country makes its own foreign policy to adapt to the international system in order to ensure the state's survival and prosperity. This very complicated process must consider a number of factors affecting foreign policy, which is in general conceived of as enterprise made from a complex process of interactions among domestic and external factors.

In the traditional approach, international relations are conducted by political units, and foreign policy normally begins where domestic policy ends.[1] Classical realists draw an analogy between states in the international arena and billiard balls: The balls constantly collide with each other, and action is caused by the interaction among nations independent of the events occurring within the states. In contrast, although neo-classical realists agree with the traditional realist view that the scope and ambition of a country's foreign policy is driven first and foremost by the international structure emerging from the material power distribution among nations, the impact of the power structure on foreign policy is indirect and complex, because systemic pressures are translated through intervening unit-level variables (e.g., decision makers' perceptions and public opinion). Thus, understanding a specific foreign policy goal requires the close examination of not merely the international, but also the domestic contexts within which foreign policy is formulated.[2]

From the neo-realist viewpoint, classical realists neglect the internal factors that should be considered as intervening variables. More concretely, the neo-realists believe that decision makers do not directly respond to external factors. The foreign policy elites listen to society's interpretations of the external threat before deciding their foreign policy course.

This paper aims to analyze the internal interpretation influencing Russian foreign policy. Among the various kinds of internal factors that exist, this paper will examine nationalism because it is believed to be one of the most significant factors influencing the perception of political elites and

---

1 Henry A. Kissinger. "Domestic Structure and Foreign Policy," *Daedalus*, Vol. 95, No. 2, 1966, p. 503.
2 Gideon Rose. "Neoclassical Realism and Theories of Foreign Policy," *World Politics*, Vol. 51, 1998.

the public alike in Russia. A review of the literature shows that a relationship exists between nationalism and international conflicts. Yet controversy arises when considering whether nationalism causes international conflicts or vice versa. In other words, is nationalism the cause or result of international conflicts? This paper aims to prove that nationalism in Russia causes conflicts with foreign countries by examining such cases as the Georgian War and the Crimean separatism in which Russia became involved.

To achieve the stated research goal, this paper will be organized as follows. The first section will review the literature on the relationship between nationalism and international conflicts and develop an analytical framework to account for the Russian cases. The second section will outline the contextual environment of Russian foreign policy and define the power relationship between Russia and the West. The third section will deal with the nationalism discourse in Russian society, and the last section will investigate the Russian offensive in both Georgia and Ukraine.

Theoretical Discussion on Nationalism and International Conflicts

According to Holsti, ideology is the intellectual framework through which national roles, images, policy, and ethical beliefs are constructed.[3] The foreign policy of a state does not seem to be free from its peculiar ideology.[4] The importance of the relationship between national identity and foreign policy received greater attention in the 1990s. Some scholars have even argued that identity and security are inseparable. Hunt argues that ideology marks the starting point in explaining the American behavior when addressing world affairs.[5] According to Kissinger, beliefs prevail over interests in the declared aims of US foreign policy. This view suggests that Americans always claim to be struggling in the name of value, not interest.[6]

---

3 Kalevi J. Holsti. *International Politics: A Framework for Analysis* (Englewood Cliffs, NJ: Prentice-Hall, 1974).

4 Walter Carlsnaes. *Ideology and Foreign Policy: Problems of Comparative Conceptualization* (Oxford: Basil Blackwell, 1986).

5 Michael Hunt. *Ideology and US Foreign Policy* (New Haven, CT: Yale University Press, 1987).

6 Henry Kissinger. *Diplomacy* (New York: Touchstone Books, 1994), p. 810.

Many theorists agree that ideology has played an important role in modern international relations. In particular, ideology has always been an integral part of Russian politics. Soviet foreign policy was explicitly ideological, and this practice lasts today. Communist ideology was replaced by nationalism. In today's Russia, nationalism is used to prop up the legitimacy of the political regime and often provides a critical source of social cohesion, especially in the midst of instable political situations. Nationalism, as the political expression of national identity, can transform a group into a nation; thus, it is ideology in a sense that it has the capability to mobilize people. Anthony Smith called nationalism an ideological motive for attaining and maintaining autonomy and unity.[7]

Ariel points out that the Kremlin has combined continuing state weakness with an increasingly assertive foreign policy. He argues that Russian elites use foreign policy as a tool to buttress domestic support and foster a threat perception that Russia is surrounded by enemies, particularly when its democratic legitimacy is deteriorating.[8] Given this view, he believes that the Russian foreign policy is vulnerable to political abuse. McFall worries that such abuse would grow as instability increases in the domestic politics Russia often faces. He warns that the uncertain political context provides opportunities for political actors to pursue strategies serving their regime maintenance and trigger international conflict and war.[9]

The literature discussed thus far reveals that unstable domestic politics lead to assertive foreign policy conduct. Political elites are easily tempted to use an adventurous foreign policy to enhance political legitimacy. In these situations, nationalism is used to draw public support for any assertive foreign policy. Developing a theoretically grounded analysis on the relationship between Russian nationalism and its foreign policy behavior requires contributions from both theories of nationalism and international relations—two areas of scholarship that have remained divided by a conceptual chasm that few have been willing to bridge.[10]

---

7   Anthony Smith. *National Identity* (London: Penguin, 1991), p. 72.
8   Cohen Ariel. "Domestic Factors Driving Russia's Foreign Policy," *Backgrounder,* No. 2084, 2007.
9   Michael McFaul. "A Precarious Peace. Domestic Politics in the Making of Russian Foreign Policy," *International Security*, Vol. 22, No. 3, 1997, p. 5.
10   F. H. Hinsley. *Nationalism and the International System* (Dobbs Ferry: Oceana Publications, 1973), p. 15.

Thus, in order to analyze the impact of nationalism on Russian foreign policy behavior, it is necessary to bridge the international relations–nationalism gap by developing a theoretical framework. This paper will seek to lay out such a framework and apply it to the widely observed resurgence of Russian nationalism in order to examine whether or not it makes Russia more prone to international conflicts. The theoretical model developed below is grounded in the neorealist approach, which focuses on the ways in which nationalism interprets threats perceived from the international system. Nationalism would be better seen as an intervening variable capable of fueling mistrust between states.

Figure 1 Analytical Framework of Foreign Policy Making

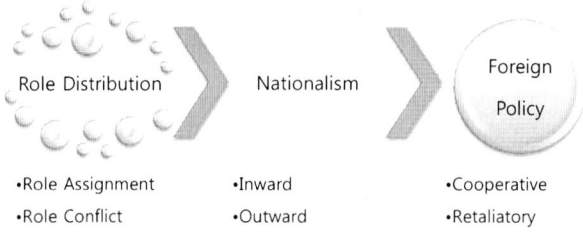

Role Distribution	Nationalism	Foreign Policy
•Role Assignment	•Inward	•Cooperative
•Role Conflict	•Outward	•Retaliatory

As Figure 1 shows, foreign policy acts as a dependent variable in two different ways. Retaliatory conduct is an assertive type of foreign policy whereas cooperative conduct means that both parties are willing to cooperate. Structural realists assume that the external factor of foreign policy is materialistic and define it as the distribution of capabilities among nations. However, this paper instead suggests that the external threat is defined in ideational terms and thus attempts to define it as the distribution of roles among them. Treating the external factor ideationally might be useful for analyzing the Russian cases. States' roles in the world order are generally seen comprising two parts: role conception and role prescription. The former refers to the foreign policymakers' own definitions of roles suitable to their state; it is their image of the appropriate orientations or functions of their state toward the external environment.[11] The latter refers to the external expectation of the state's role, indicating the country's placement in the international system that other countries consider appropriate.

---

11 K. J. Holsti. "National Role Conceptions in the Study of Foreign Policy," *International Studies Quarterly*, Vol. 14, 1970, p. 245.

In this regard, roles are self-defined and partly imposed from the outside. Alexander Wendt argues that states do not necessarily have the ability to choose their roles freely, particularly in cases where the level of interactions with other states is high.[12] Role conflicts are likely to arise when the role that a state seeks to enact comes into conflict with the role that other states seek to impose on it. In other words, a state's role conception might conflict with the role prescription of another state.

For instance, the United States seeks to disseminate democracy and human rights by recasting Russia as a failed modernizer—a role that conflicts with Russia's own role as a great power. This role conflict represents a threat not just to Russia's material security, but also to its ideational security. The result has been the rise of Russian nationalism that was largely anti-Western in character. Role conflicts determine foreign policy types through the prism of nationalism. In this mechanism, national identity has a guiding impact on foreign policy.

This model suggests that the type of foreign policy is the result of an ideational threat from the outside and presumes that the threats from the outside are ideational, not just physical in nature. Stephan Van Evera argues that nationalism becomes a strong motivating factor for the pursuit of aggressive foreign policies toward that other state. According to him, two kinds of nationalism emerge: either a purely self-liberating enterprise or a hegemonic enterprise.[13] Whether nationalism makes a state more prone to international conflict might depend on the nature of ideology—namely, inward or outward. Outward nationalism, which pursues a hegemonic position, will inevitably cause clashes with foreign countries.

Russia's Relations with the West since the Collapse of the Soviet Union

The great power role has long been central to Russians' strategic thought. In recent centuries, Russia has always been an empire; the Soviet Union was no exception. The search for a great power status has long been a national mission for Russians. The first line of Russia's national anthem puts it succinctly: "Russia is our sacred power."

---

12 Alexander Wendt. *Social Theory of International Politics* (Cambridge: Cambridge University Press, 1999), p. 228.
13 Stephen Van Evera. "Hypotheses on Nationalism and War," Michael E. Brown (ed.), *Nationalism and Ethic Conflict* (Cambridge: The MIT Press, 1997), p. 278.

However, Russia has had to struggle to meet the challenges posed by the West throughout its history, and the Western challenge continued after the end of Cold War. The United States began heralding liberal democracy, human rights, and market economy to the post-communist states and imposed on Russia a set of neoliberal values that differed from the traditional Russian understanding. Russian political leaders initially attempted to modernize the state system with political and economic reforms. The West saw Russia struggle with its modernization and promised to support the reforms.

Until the mid-2000s, bilateral cooperation between Russia and the West, on the whole, showed high reciprocity in nature. This means that Russia's increased cooperation toward the West was met with West's increased cooperation toward Russia and vice versa. The cooperative relationship reached two peaks: in 1993 and 1998. In 1993, the Russian government launched its market reform, the so-called shock therapy, and desperately needed assistance from the West. However, the painful results of market reforms led to disappointments toward the West. Benefitting from this circumstance, Zhirinovsky's extreme right Liberal Democratic Party and the nationalist-inclined Communist Party made great strides in the December 1993 elections. The whole process strengthened connections in the minds of the Russians between pro-Western reform and economic hardship and social disorder.

In subsequent years, the relationship between Russia and the United States became more fragile due to political and security issues. In 1994, the Russian government undertook a large-scale armed intervention into the Chechen Republic despite opposition from the West. Throughout 1995, international disagreements over policy in Yugoslavia and NATO's plans for eastward expansion generated hostile sentiments in the Yeltsin administration.

The popular belief is that Yeltsin took a pro-Western alignment in his first term, but shifted his approach in his second term. However, the empirical results illustrate that, despite Yeltsin's rhetoric, his cooperative conduct continued throughout his time in office. In particular, the IMF moratorium forced the Yeltsin administration to cooperate with the United States. Overcoming the financial crisis in the late 1990s caused an upturn in Russia's cooperation behavior. The economic situation required the government to cooperate closely with the United States. Meanwhile, the September 11 attacks in 2001 gave Putin an opportunity to get closer to the United States. He made a commitment to help the United States in the global war against terrorism. Thus, Russia became an indispensable partner of the United States by providing assistance in logistics and the information necessary for invading Afghanistan.

Russia economically recovered in the 2000s as a result of the continuously rising oil prices. Putin's worldview and his perception of Russia's place on the world stage have undergone marked changes. By the mid-2000s, the ruling elite in Russia sought to regain its lost status as a great power. The Russian people, who have endured the post-communist transformation, hailed the shift in the Russian foreign policy. This circumstance completely contradicted American expectations. From the Western viewpoint, Russia became a failed modernizer.

Nationalism Discourse in the Russian Society

Two analytically distinct concepts of Russian nationalism exist: statist and civilizational. The former represents state approaches, discourses and ideology outlined in Kremlin statements, presidential addresses, and foreign policy doctrines. The latter is conceived by Russian society.

The break-up of the Soviet Union sped up the emergence of nationalism in Russia. The share of ethnic Russians in the population grew from a bare majority of 52% in the multinational Soviet Union to a predominant 80% in the Russian Federation. This newfound majority status naturally boosted national and cultural reassertion. Furthermore, Russian nationalism was heightened by the creation of Russian minorities dispersed throughout adjacent countries. Twenty-five million Russians became minorities overnight. Civilizational nationalism aims to defend the cultural, moral, and historical aspects of the distinct Russian way of life. Whereas statist nationalism emphasizes the statehood, civilizational nationalism stresses a sense of national solidarity. This portrays Russia as a besieged fortress.

During the Putin era, the potential for civilizational nationalism to influence the elite discourse has increased. First, the process of foreign policy making has become centralized, being restricted to a very narrow circle of trusted advisers and presidential administration. This opened opportunities for personal connections and other indirect forms of influence from which civilizational nationalists might unduly benefit.

Nationalism in the Russian government is by nature moderate relative to civilizational nationalism in the society because its aim is not the expression of nationalism per se, but its utilization for regime goals. On the one hand, the Kremlin periodically co-opts and mobilizes nationalism. On the other, it repeatedly suppresses nationalism when it threatens the political stability. Such an approach of the ruling elite prevents civilizational nationalism from becoming an influential, independent force in Russian politics.[14]

Under Putin, statist nationalism has by and large been dominant in foreign policy making. For the political elite, statehood and stability were important as equated the idea of Russia with Russian citizenry, not the ethnic Russian nation. Statist nationalism is articulated in the doctrine of sovereign democracy. Surkov, who invented sovereign democracy, argues that recognizable national models of democracy exist in France, Britain, and Germany, all with a mix of the universal and specific. The idea of the sovereign democracy aimed to limit foreign interference in Russia's political system in response to colored revolutions breaking out in the post-Soviet space.[15]

Nevertheless, the illiberal and nationalistic emphasis is implicit rather than explicit. Putin continuously declares that Russia's national interests are economic modernization and competitiveness. Russia is eager to be recognized as a normal country meeting world standards of democracy while maintaining its own sovereign sphere. Despite the moderate feature of sovereign democracy, many argue that anti-Western nationalism has been moving from the margins to the mainstream of state discourse. Nationalism ineluctably began to influence Russian foreign policy. The assertive and even aggressive Russian foreign policy that emerged in recent years has been associated with ideational underpinnings that have sought to challenge Western liberalism. The state's approaches to nationalism have changed in its interactions with more aggressive, civilizational nationalism, driving it to adopt an assertive foreign policy.

Figure 2 shows the rise of nationalism in Russian society. It reached three peaks—in 2001, 2008, and today—indicating that the beginning of the Putin era, the Georgian War, and the Ukrainian Crisis are closely related with the emergence of Russian nationalism. Among the three events, the latter two cases are issues of foreign policy.

---

14 Richard Sakwa. "New Cold War or Twenty Years' Crisis? Russia and International Politics," International Affairs, Vol. 84, No. 2, 2008.
15 Luke March. "Is Nationalism Rising in Russian Foreign Policy? The Case of Georgia," *Demokratizatsiya*, p. 191.

Figure 2 "What do you think about the idea 'Russia for Russians'?"
(n=1600)

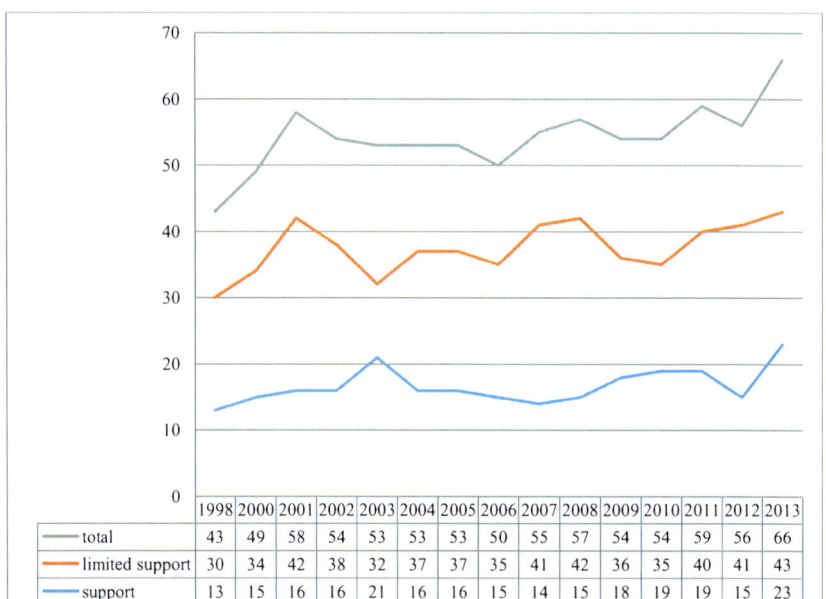

	1998	2000	2001	2002	2003	2004	2005	2006	2007	2008	2009	2010	2011	2012	2013
total	43	49	58	54	53	53	53	50	55	57	54	54	59	56	66
limited support	30	34	42	38	32	37	37	35	41	42	36	35	40	41	43
support	13	15	16	16	21	16	16	15	14	15	18	19	19	15	23

Source: Levada Center, *Russian Public Opinion 2012–13*, Moscow 2013.

Cases of the Georgian War and Ukrainian Crisis

The Georgian War was Russia's first international war after the collapse of the Soviet Union, and the same kind of military conflict is imminent with Ukraine. Why does Russia conduct such offensive foreign policy toward its neighboring countries? What role does Russian nationalism play in the Russian–Georgian War? The role of nationalism in the Russia–Georgian War of August 2008 has been largely ignored. By the summer of 2008, an increasingly nationalistic and revisionist Russia rebelled against the world order dominated by the West.[16] Russia's diplomatic recognition of Abkhazia and South Ossetia in defiance of the Western positions can be seen as the tipping point when Russia began to substantiate its rhetoric and

---

16 Roland Asmus. *A Little War that Shook the World: Georgia, Russia, and the Future of the West* (London: Bloomsbury Publishing PLC, 2009), p. 14.

export highly nationalistic internal values in an attempt to revise the post-Cold War order.[17]

The Russian–Georgian War demonstrated that civilizational nationalism affected Russia's foreign policy. The goal of the war was to expand Russian influence in the post-Soviet space and punish Georgia, which attempted to benefit from the Color Revolution and NATO expansion. In the Putin era, the domestic mobilization of civilizational nationalism increased, demonstrating an unprecedented spill-over from the domestic to the foreign policy realms.[18] Since 2009, there has been a partial return to normalcy. The Russian elite seemed aware of the dangers of aggressive nationalism escaping their control and have sought to return to non-nationalist rhetoric. However, this is likely to remain a superficial reset that does not circumvent the likelihood of nationalism increasingly affecting Russian foreign policy. This expectation has materialized in the Ukrainian crisis. Russians have long been confounded by Ukrainian independence because the origins of the Russian state are within Kievan Rus.

Faced with the global financial crisis in 2009, Putin came up with his priority foreign policy project: Eurasian integration. The concept of the Eurasian Economic Union and the steps taken toward its implementation thus far reflect a trend toward the reintegration of the post-Soviet economic space. Many Western politicians and experts perceive the Eurasian Economic Union project as an attempt to resurrect the Soviet Union.[19]

In 2014, Moscow was supposed to focus on finalizing preparations for launching the Eurasian Economic Union. However, in early 2014, Russia's foreign policy direction changed dramatically. Responding to the series of events in Ukraine that led to the ouster of President Yanukovych by protesters in Maidan square in Kiev, Moscow incorporated Crimea into the Russian Federation. Russia again found itself in a confrontation with the United States and its allies.[20]

---

17 Luke March. "Is Nationalism Rising in Russian Foreign Policy? The Case of Georgia," *Demokratizatsiya*, p. 188.

18 Luke March. "Is Nationalism Rising in Russian Foreign Policy? The Case of Georgia," *Demokratizatsiya*, p. 189.

19 Pyotr Stegny. "Russia's Foreign Policy: Searching for a New Paradigm," Kadri Liik (ed.) *Russia's Pivot to Eurasia* (London: European Council on Foreign Relations, 2014), p. 36.

20 Dmitri Trenin. "Drivers of Russia's Foreign Policy," Kadri Liik (ed.) *Russia's Pivot to Eurasia* (London: European Council on Foreign Relations, 2014), p. 36.

This analysis of nationalism in foreign policy making in Russia draws the following conclusion: The role distribution between Russia and the West is an external factor affecting Russia's foreign policy making. Role prescription by the West can be perceived as a threat to Russian values and interests; thus, the role imposed by the West can invite resistance among the Russian elite and people. As a result, nationalism can either exaggerate or alleviate the threat perception. In the cases of the Georgian War and Ukrainian Crisis, nationalism exacerbated the position of Russia toward the West.

This work was supported by the National Research Foundation of Korea Grant funded by the Korean Government (NRF-2013S1A3A2054311).

Russia as Provider of Energetic Resources for Europe and Korea: Problems and Approaches to Solutions

Werner Gumpel

Russia is one of the biggest energy exporters of the world. Its largest sales market is the European Union, especially Germany. But also the states of Northeast Asia are getting more and more important for the Russian sales strategy. Thus Russia has turned into an important partner as regards the economic development of the countries concerned, which has not only positive but also negative consequences. These consequences will be discussed subsequently, with a first analysis of the situation in Europe and especially in Germany as well as an ensuing reference to the Northeast Asian countries. In this context the People's Republic of China and the Republic of Korea will be in the main focus.

1. The present situation

Russia is not only an important provider of crude oil, but especially of natural gas, too. The European Union imports 27 per cent of its gas requirements from this country, topped by Germany with a rate of even 38 per cent. This means a profound dependence on Russia on the energy sector. This has not only an economic but also an immense political significance. The most important aim of a national energy policy must be the guarantee of secure energy supplies, both in political as well as in technical respects. In both cases the situation has been repeatedly problematic in the past. Gas exports from Russia have been used again and again as political weapon against the Ukraine and Lithuania – long before the political turbulences. On the other hand, Western politicians have threatened to reduce the gas imports from Russia in case of an open military intervention in the Ukraine. With the given dependence on Russian supplies Germany cannot be interested in such a measure, the more so as there are no short-term alternatives for the Russian supplies. As the situation of the other EU countries is similar to the German in view of the dependence on Russian supplies, the EU commission will be reluctant to impose sanctions against Russia.

2. *Alternatives to Russia*

The EU countries – whose demand for natural gas increases by 6.2 per cent annually - are indeed looking for alternatives in order to reduce the dependence on Russia. This could be achieved in three ways:

- Increasing the energy efficiency which is – without doubt – a general aim of the energy policy. In this field enormous progress has already been made in the past decades, so that the existing possibilities have been respectively are used to a very large extent.
- Exploiting resources that have not been used so far with the help of fracking. In this field Germany shows a considerable potential, however, there are strong objections especially by environmentalists as well as fears among the population concerning possible damages caused by earthmoving or explosions and health damages due to the contamination of water and soil. If and to what extent fracking is politically possible remains to be seen.
- A third possibility is the diversification of provision. In this case – apart from some North African states such as Algeria and Qatar – above all the Central Asian states have come into focus. The first, however, must liquefy their natural gas for the transport to Europe, implying the building of suitable plants and – consequently – a high capital requirement. The countries that depend most on the Russian natural gas are situated in East and Central Europe and do not provide of terminals for liquefied gas.

A possible future supplier of natural gas to the south of Europe is Turkmenistan. This country is interested in finding more purchasers for its natural gas in Europe in order to diversify its exports. It plans to boost its exports to 180 billion cubic meters per year. So far it depends almost completely on the demand from Russia. Therefore it is very interested in opening up Europe as sales market for crude oil and natural gas. Unfortunately the country finds itself in a problematic situation: two thirds of the exports have to pass the Russian territory by using the Russian pipelines. A further obstacle in this situation is the fact that the natural gas from Turkmenistan is not only sold to the Russian Federation but also to other former Soviet republics, as it was the case when the Soviet Union still existed. In order to avoid this, the country plans to build pipelines without passing through Russia.[1] Only if this plan succeeds will it be possible to reduce the dependency on Russia.

Azerbaijan, too, exports natural gas to Europe and covers with 10 billion cubic meters two per cent of the European annual requirements amounting to 560 billion cubic meters. In comparison, Russia delivers the fifteen-fold quantity. There is, however, every indication that *Azerbaijan* endeavors to exploit new natural gas reserves and to show increased presence on the European market. Such a project is the gas field of Schach Deniz. From there the gas is supposed to be transported via the Trans-Anatolian pipeline and the Trans-Adriatic pipeline to Europe and China, too. To the south of the island Cyprus Israel plans the exploitation of the natural gas fields in the Mediterranean Sea. From there, too, gas should flow to Europe. The trans-Caspian pipeline, which leads from Aktau to Baku and from there via the Georgian Tbilisi to the Turkish Erzurum, has been operated since the mid-nineties of the past century. From there the gas flows through Turkey to Europe. Libya delivers its gas via Algiers to Italy, with the help of the "Greenstream" pipeline, which is situated at a depth of 1127 meters below sea level. Not to forget the fact that Iran is connected to the Turkish pipeline system via a pipeline in the East-Anatolian Erzurum. All this shows that the Russians have to face a strong competition on the European continent which will increase further. In the medium term a decrease of Russian gas deliveries to Europe is to be expected.

For Germany it is actually decisive that with the construction of the so-called northern pipeline, which leads from the Jamal peninsula in the far north of Russia via Wyborg and below the Baltic Sea to the German Baltic coast, the so far existing dependence on transit services provided by the Ukraine and Poland have been reduced considerably.

For Russia the situation concerning the deliveries to Europe worsens due to the conflict between the Russian and the Ukrainian part of the population in the Ukraine. So far the Ukraine is the most important transit country for the natural gas determined for Europe. In case the Russians actually stop their gas deliveries that flow through the pipelines there – a

---

1 Cf. as well as Aserbeidschan and Algeria: Hajtun, Aleksej: Gas na jushnom flange evropy. In: Nesavisimaja gazeta Online (www.ng.ru/energiya/ 2014-03-24/9south_gas.html?print=Y_

threat that was made in earnest – this will not only leave the Ukraine without natural gas but it would also be a heavy blow for the European gas consumers. If, however, the transit pipelines through the Ukraine can be used further, but the gas supply is cut off for the Ukraine, the Ukrainians will probably not hesitate to tap the transit pipelines. This has happened several times in the past.[2] Even private individuals have tapped the Russian pipelines again and again, with explosions happening more than once.

3. The German interest

If Europe succeeds in diversifying its supplies in the long run, Russia will have to find ways to compensate the market shares lost in Europe by conquering the Asian markets. However, it will not be prepared to give up the European and especially the German market. Germany is the biggest purchaser of Russian energy sources and – vice versa – Germany is the most important import partner. It is Russia's biggest trade partner, after the Netherlands and China. Moreover it is the most important supplier of industrial goods and the German economy belongs to the biggest investors in the country. On the other hand, Russian investors invest a great deal of money in Germany. For these reasons Russia remains interested in the German market and good political relations to Germany – in spite of all political turbulences. The dependence is thus not unilateral, but mutual and the economic interests of both countries actually are the same. Policy has to take this into account. Lenin once said that policy was "the concentrated expression of economy". This is true in this case, too.

Germany doesn't stand alone as far as its interests are concerned. Other EU members such as for example Poland as well as leading EU politicians demand a stronger influence of the EU on the energy policy of the member states and the creation of a "European Energy Union". Contracts on gas supplies from Russia should – according to their opinion – be negotiated together in future times. The expectations are a smaller dependence on Russia and more favorable prices.[3] Considering the very different interests of the EU states, it is, however, very doubtful that such a union will come about. For Russia it would be one further obstacle for the presence

---

2 Concering the problematic nature of the gas transit s. Nesavisimaja Gazeta, online-edition (www.ng.ru/economicx/2014-04-28/1_gas.hmtl?print=Y)
3 Frankfurter Allgemeine Zeitung, 02. 05. 2014

on the European market. Russian research institutes reckon that the contribution of hydrocarbons to the Russian GDP (gross domestic product) will change dramatically in the years to come. A decline of the corresponding exports by 15 – 20 per cent has already been predicted for the year 2015. This tendency has already been reflected in the past years. Thus, the capacity of the "Blue Stream" pipeline, which delivers gas through the Black Sea to Turkey and from there partly to Europe, is utilized at less than 5 per cent.[4]

Under the given circumstances it is only too understandable that Russia endeavors to open up new markets in Northeast Asia. For this purpose another necessity has to be mentioned: a part of the reserves in the European part of the country are slowly running out. Now it is about opening up the partly or completely unexploited resources in the "far east" of the country. According to Russia this will be worthwhile because "the region Northeast Asia as a whole represents a practically unlimited market for energetic goods and services".[5] With this economic goal a demographic one goes closely together. The "far east" of Russia records a relatively sharp decrease in population caused by migration. The census in the year 2013 revealed a decrease in population of six per cent.[6] Where the Russians go, the Chinese come. The Russian government's aim is that – with the development of new resources – Russian immigrants come to the sparsely populated regions. For that purpose, however, an adequate infrastructure has to be built up first. Consequently that means that "in reality the Chinese factor – and not only that , but also the South Korean and the Japanese – are affiliated with the perspective of the economic development and, if you like, not only with the economic but also with the political future of this Russian region.[7]

---

4 Jupkin, Mchail: Prognos rasvitija energetiki mira do 2040 goda. In: Nesavisimaja gazeta Online,(www.ng.ru/ng_energija/2014-02-11/11)_ razvilka.html? print=Y.html

5 Mastenanov, Aleksej: Energopartnerstvo v Severo-Wostotschnoj Asii. In: Nesavisimaja gazeta Online, (www.ng.ru/ng_energiya/2013-02-12/11-korea.html?print-Y)

6 Nikiforov, Oleg: Rossijskij gas v KNR: poisk reschenij. In: Nesavisimaja gazeta (www.ng.ru/ng_energiya/2013-06-11/13_knr_gaz.html?print-Y)

7 Ibid.

4. China's part

Russia's major interest is focused on the *People's Republic of China*, which has an essential interest in obtaining gas from Russia. At the moment it is covering 4 per cent of its gas requirements by imports from Russia, a share it would like to increase to 10 per cent by the year 2020. For that purpose new routes for the gas transport are required. In addition, China has a great interest in increasing the imports of crude oil from Russia. The share of oil and oil products amounts to 70 per cent of the Chinese imports from Russia. In the medium term, as "Gazprom" Chairman Aleksey Miller put it prior to President Putin's visit to China in May 2014, "the demand from China will equal that of the supplies to Europe".[8] In this context China ensured 20 years of secured supplies by granting a credit of 15 billion Dollars for building a pipeline.[9] Nevertheless, there are recurrent disputes between China and Russia as far as the pricing by "Gazprom", "Rosneft" and "Transneft", the big Russian monopolist companies, is concerned. The Central Asian states sell their gas much cheaper than "Gazprom" and are therefore competitors if it is about price policy, even if their gas flows to other Chinese regions than the Russian. In the course of the past decade China's share in the gas exports of the Central Asian states has been ever increasing. In the years 2009 and 2010 a number of pipelines of various capacities were laid from Kazakhstan and Turkmenistan to China without any involvement of the Russian companies. This shows that these countries are trying to free themselves more and more from the dependency on Russia. The competitive situation between those countries and Russia will even increase in the decades to come. China is taking advantage of this situation in order to negotiate the most favorable conditions for its supplies. Uzbekistan and Turkmenistan have de facto already left the Russian sphere of influence and pursue an independent energy policy. Tadzhikistan and Kirgizia, however, maintain their cooperation with Russia, as they expect a stabilization of their complex economic and internal situation. As far as their foreign policy is concerned, they both have increasingly closer relations to China.[10]

---

8 Kommersant, 19. 05. 2014 (www.kommersant.ru/doc/2474253
9 Kommersant, 28.02.2010 (kommersant.ru/doc/18882127/print)
10 Shiljzov, Sergej: Neftegasovaja schvatka v Zentraljnoj Asii. In Nesavisimaja gazeta (www.ng.ru/ng_energija/2013-06-11/12_gaz.html?print=Y)

As for their endeavors for the East Asian energy markets the Russians make use of both bilateral as well as multilateral negotiations and contracts. Additionally they try to realize substantial energy projects on a common basis.

5. South Korea – Russia's new target

Russia's economic interest in the Republic of Korea also consists of its integration into the Russian sales markets for natural gas and crude oil. South Korea imports 90 per cent of its crude oil requirements from other countries, such as Iran and Iraq, a fact that has awakened Russia's interest in the Korean market. South Korea is thus described as "one of the most important potential partners" in the Russian media. Both Russia's and South Korea's interests as far as the supply of natural gas is concerned, are absolutely identical.[11] The strategy applied corresponds mainly to that applied for China. Of course the criteria differ in view of the country's size, its economic power and its total population, and thus of the possible quantity of sales. For Korea, however, the enlargement of the energetic relations to Russia could actually mean an increase of its growth forces. In this context it is not only South Korea that Russia bears in mind, but also the communist North Korea. Corresponding plans have been developed since the year 1989. This development goes together with the exploitation of the gas supplies in Yakutia and the Shelf of Sakhalin, which should serve for its domestic demand as well as for the export via pipelines and, liquefied, on ships. At that time the gas from the fields in Yakutia should be directed via China and North Korea to the Republic of Korea. The collapse of the Soviet Union brought the project to its temporary end. In the years 1993 to 1995 it was resumed under Japanese research cooperation. Russian and Japanese institutes worked out a master plan for the energetic development of East Siberia and the Far East in view of future exports into the countries of the region Asia – Pacific Ocean. The existing plan is still seen as the basic Russian energy strategy.

The master plan was met with lively interest in the region. Three big international projects came into being, among them the project concerning

---

11 Nikiforov, Oleg: Jushnaja Korea moshet statj kljutschevym energopartnjorom Rossii. In: Nesavisimaja gazeta online, 26.10.2012 (www.ng.ru/printed/274949)

an export pipeline from the Irkutsk region via China to North Korea and from there to South Korea. Chinese and Korean gas companies were then also part of these projects. The construction works lasted until the year 2004. The project intends an annual supply of 20 billion cubic meters of gas to Chinese customers and of 10 billion cubic meters to South Korean purchasers. A further pipeline should deliver Russian gas to Japan.[12] According to Russian calculations the construction of the gas pipeline would enable South Korea to reduce the price for the natural gas presently bought from the countries of the Near East by 30 per cent.[13]

The possibility of delivering Russian natural gas to the Republic of Korea via a pipeline was again studied in the year 2000. Based on these studies new plans were developed which were confirmed in a regulation of the Russian Energy Ministry in the year 2007. "Gazprom" is coordinating the program. The gas pipeline from East Siberia to South Korea can thus materialize.

The Russian gas supplies will alleviate the energy poverty of the country and consequently have a great economic significance. Their transport, however, goes through the territory of a state with which the Republic of Korea is de jure still at war. That means that one of the three basic principles of energy economy, namely that of political security of supply, is not guaranteed. North Korea has the advantage of collecting the transit charges, a stimulus for cooperation, but its behavior in the past raises fears that it will use the pipeline as a political instrument, if this seems appropriate. The reduction of South Korea's energy shortage with the help of Russian supplies is probably not the best solution, because an incalculable political risk remains.

In conclusion it can be said that the market for hydro carbons is dynamic not only because of the increasing demand of industrial and developing countries, but also – to a considerable extent – because of the changing Russian strategy of partly shifting its exports towards China, Korea, Japan and India. This enables those countries to forge new paths as far as securing their import demand is concerned.

---

12 Mastepanov, Aleksej: Energopartnerstvo v Severo-Vostotschnoj Asii, a. a. O
13 Nikiforov, Oleg, l.c. (loco citato)

III)

Cambodia as Exemplar of Reunification for Korea?

Cambodia – A Case of Negotiated Reunification

Gottfried-Karl Kindermann

Looking back at 39 years of the highly rewarding cooperation of the University of Munich with Korean Universities and research institutions, foremost with the renowned Yonsei-University, I do remember that many of our joint conferences have dealt with issues related to Korean or German unification. Doing so, one is faced with the fundamental question which types of re-unification of previously divided nations have there been in the post-World War II era? There are at least three such cases:

The first is reunification by conquest, as has been the case in Vietnam when South Vietnam was conquered by the armies and guerillas of North Vietnam in April of 1975.

The second case is Germany, where the government of one part of that divided country was overwhelmed by the revolutionary vigor of its own population and forced by it to commit political suicide by consenting to free elections that sealed the fate of East Germany's dictatorship and opened the door to a peaceful and democratic form of reunification.

The third case is that of Cambodia, where the governments of two antagonistic systems and all major political parties were put under a temporary trusteeship of the United Nations in order to elaborate jointly a united and democratic system of government. At the same time, the hegemonic imperialism of Vietnam, aiming at the domination of Cambodia and all of Indochina, could be contained.

CAMBODIA UNTIL the RED KHMER

Cambodia, a relatively little known country in the West, had formed in the 12-th century a culturally splendid empire, where the Vishnu and Shiva cult coexisted with forms of Hinayana Buddhism. With the temple city of Angkor Wat they created the most impressive monument of Khmer art, culture and religion. In subsequent centuries Cambodia frequently became a victim of incursions by its powerful neighbors, Thailand and Vietnam, who often fought each other on Cambodian soil. In desperation, Cambodia's king Ang Duong in 1853 appealed to Emperor Napoleon III for assistance. France however used Cambodia's appeal for imposing upon the Khmer kingdom a system of French colonial domination.

During the American war in Vietnam, that started in 1964/65, Cambodian territories were often ruthlessly impaired by military operations of U.S. and North Vietnamese forces. With only limited success, Cambodia's ruler Prince Norodom Sihanouk endeavored to maintain his country's neutrality. But in March of 1970 he was ousted from his position of leadership by Cambodia's pro-American Prime Minister General Lon Nol and his Deputy Prince Sirik Mata. This new government found itself soon involved in war with the Communist Khmer Rouge who managed to conquer Phnom Penh, the capital city of Cambodia two weeks prior to the capitulation of South Vietnam.

What followed was a reign of unprecedented terror by the Khmer Rouge, who established in Cambodia the world's most totalitarian system of government, based on a crude comprehension of Marxism and aspects of early Maoism. It is estimated that about 26 percent of the population perished as a result of torture, overwork, malnutrition, exhaustion and execution. In addition, the Khmer Rouge drove Cambodia itself into a fierce territorial dispute with Vietnam that caused Cambodia to seek closer relations with China.

TWO INTER-COMMUNIST WARS

Peking was outraged by Vietnam's inclusion into the Soviet dominated economic organization COMECON and even more so by a Soviet-Vietnamese treaty of friendship and cooperation of November 3rd 1978 by which China was geostrategically wedged in between the Soviet Union in the North and Vietnam in the South. Backed by its treaty with Moscow, Vietnam only one month later launched a carefully prepared military offensive against Cambodia, a quasi-ally of China. Jointly with Vietnam's invading army, a Cambodian force calling itself "Cambodian United Front for National Salvation" marched into Cambodia where it immediately initiated a massive propaganda campaign against the Red Khmer and their outrageous crimes against their country's own population. Very much to the dismay of the Chinese, calling itself People's Republic of Cambodia, the new regime announced it would contribute to a kind of union of the three Indochina states: Vietnam, Laos, and Cambodia. Seen from the perspective of China's national interest, Vietnam's conquest and satellization of Cambodia would indeed have transformed Indochina into a relatively strong power and Soviet ally in Southeast Asia.

Regardless of Vietnam's alliance with the Soviet Union, China on January 31, 1979 launched a military campaign against Vietnam which Peking called in Chinese zheng Fa or "punitive expedition", formerly the designation of punitive wars which Chinese Emperors used in order to discipline disobedient border tribes. But possessing a plentitude of captured American arms and other equipment, and having learned from the military experience of nine years of war with France and ten years with the United States, the Vietnamese proved to be formidable adversaries. China thus had to stop the war after one month only, without having achieved any visible success.

THE ROLE of the SOVIET UNION

In addition, Peking had to worry about the Soviet invasion of Afghanistan, one of the territorial neighbors of China, and had to be concerned about the fact that Vietnam had leased former American military bases - such as Kam Ranh Bay - to the Soviet Union, a fact that worried other states relying upon unimpeded shipping in the South China Sea.

The Soviet Union however played a rather constructive role in this many-sided constellation. In addition, paying a state visit to China in 1989, Gorbachev was confronted with three basic demands as preconditions for terminating two decades of the Sino-Soviet cold war :

First: Withdrawal of Soviet troops from Afghanistan;
Second: Ending Soviet material support for Vietnam's hegemonic policy in Indochina;
Third: Reducing the Soviet Union's military deployment along the Sino-Soviet borders.

On behalf of the Soviet Union, Gorbachev accepted those unilateral and uncompensated demands, which included a very substantial reduction of Soviet aid for Vietnam's policies in Indochina. And this became a highly significant determinant of subsequent developments in Cambodia. At the occasion of his state visit to China, a Sino-Soviet agreement confirming the normalization of state and party relations between those two powers had been signed. In article 5 of that agreement, both powers advocate the complete withdrawal of Vietnamese forces from Cambodia and the national reintegration of that country under effective international supervision.

CAMBODIA`S DIVISION

Cambodia itself was at that time divided in two unequal parts. The largest part was ruled by the Communist but anti-Red Khmer and pro-Vietnamese government of Hun Sen, while a smaller part of Cambodia, especially territories adjacent to neighboring Thailand, were controlled by a tripartite coalition headed by Prince Norodom Sihanouk and composed of his Royalist Party FUNCINPEC (Front Uni Pour un Cambodge Indépendent, Neutre, Pacifique et Cooperatif), Son Sann's Liberal Buddhist Party, and the Khmer Rouge, that had been inaugurated on June 22, 1982. This second government of Cambodia called itself "National Government of Cambodia" (NGC). In 1982 the tripartite resistance government was admitted at the U.N. as legal representative of the Cambodian state and people, while its adversary, the pro-Vietnamese "State of Cambodia" was initially supported only by the so called "socialist" member states of the United Nations.

Perceiving the ideological background of the reserved and even hostile attitude of a majority of U.N. members, Hun Sen's State of Cambodia reacted by initiating in April 1989 a total revision of its Communist government system. Cambodia was even declared to be a democratic state with a multi-party system, limited private ownership, limited liberalization of domestic and foreign trade and a neutral foreign policy. In addition, Buddhism was declared to be the "state religion" of Cambodia. Amnesty International pointed, however, to the absence of the rule of law as a factor limiting the value and effectiveness of the above mentioned innovations.

On October 8, 1987 the pro-Vietnamese People's Republic of Cambodia announced a five-point proposal for a political solution of the Cambodian issue. According to it, Phnom Penh declared its willingness to discuss the future of Cambodia with Prince Sihanouk and the other leaders of the tripartite resistance coalition. Soon thereafter Prince Sihanouk and Hun Sen met for the first time in person in France with the understanding that this was just the beginning. Hun Sen, apparently with the permission of the Vietnamese government, categorically stated that the Vietnamese government had irreversibly decided to withdraw its armed forces from Cambodia.

UNTAC and STRATEGY of MULTILATERALISM

After a great number of intermediate bilateral and multilateral contacts and exchanges on the Cambodian issue, a first "Jakarta Informal Meeting on Cambodia" (JIM I.) assembled in the presidential palace in Bogor Indonesia, and hosted by the Indonesian government, convened from July 25 to July 28, 1988.

As Ali Alatas, the Foreign Minister of Indonesia put it, the purpose of that JIM was: "to provide the framework for informal discussions among the parties directly involved and other concerned countries in the search for a comprehensive, just and durable solution of the "Kampuchean Problem". Three other JIM-Conferences followed. JIM IV. of September 1990 produced a breakthrough that was named "the miracle of Jakarta". The Cambodian parties agreed to form a united Supreme National Council and agreed on the adoption of a statement of the five permanent members of the U.N. Security Council in New York for elaborating a basic structure for a forthcoming general settlement of the Cambodian problem.

The legally decisive document, however, was the "Final Act of the Paris Conference" signed on October 23, 1991 by the representatives of the Indochina states, China, the Soviet Union, Great Britain, France, Japan, Canada, Australia, the ASEAN states, a few other states and the Secretary General of the United Nations, Perez de Cuellar. The main purpose of this historic conference was defined as follows :

"Desiring to restore and maintain peace in Cambodia, to promote national reconciliation and ensure the right of self-determination of the Cambodian people through fair and free elections, [...]

Noting the formation in Jakarta on 10 September 1990 of the Supreme National Council of Cambodia as the unique legitimate body and source of authority in Cambodia in which, through the transitional period, national sovereignty and unity are enshrined, and which represents Cambodia externally,

Welcoming the unanimous election in Peking on 17 July 1991, of H.R.H. Prince Norodom Sihanouk as the President of the Supreme National Council,

Recognizing that an enhanced United Nations role requires the establishment of a United Nations Transitional Authority < UNTAC > with civilian and military components, which will act with full respect for the national sovereignty of Cambodia [...] have agreed as follows:

The signatories invite the United Nations Security Council to establish a United Nations Transitional Authority in Cambodia (hereafter referred to as "UNTAC") with civilian and military components under the direct responsibility of the Secretary-General of the United Nations. For this purpose the Secretary-General will designate a special representative to act on his behalf."

The most sensitive issue dealt with in this document is the relation between UNTAC and the Supreme National Council of Cambodia, headed by Prince Sihanouk. In this regard the Paris Agreement states in Article 6: "The SNC hereby delegates to the United Nations all powers necessary to ensure the implementation of this Agreement, as described in annex 1."

And according to that annex, the SNC offers advice to UNTAC, "which will comply with this advice provided there is a consensus among the members of the SNC and provided this advice is consistent with the objectives of the present agreement. [...] If there is no consensus among the members of the SNC [...] the President (Sihanouk) will be entitled to make the decision on what advice to offer to UNTAC. [...] UNTAC will comply with the advice, provided it is consistent with the objectives of the present agreement. In case the President (Sihanouk) should not be in a position to act, his power to act would be transferred to the Secretary-General's Special Representative who may take the necessary action.

According to the Paris Agreement, all civil police in Cambodia would work under UNTAC supervision and UNTAC was entitled other law enforcement and judicial processes throughout Cambodia. One of UNTAC's most important but also most difficult assignments concerned the implementation and control of measures designed to encourage and to enable the development of a democratic system of government starting with voter education programs, ensuring free access to the media and investigating complaints of electoral irregularities. The Paris Agreement on Cambodia envisages "a system of liberal democracy on the basis of pluralism", providing "periodic and genuine elections" as well as an independent judiciary, empowered to enforce the rights provided under the constitution.

UNTAC's military assignments included the imposition, control and verification of armistice agreements, to control and to register police forces and their equipment. UNTAC's military units were to organize the disposition and cantonment of the military units of the various Cambodian parties. Another important mission concerned the verification of the withdrawal of foreign forces still stationed on the soil of Cambodia and terminating their supply with foreign arms. A very important task, especially for Cambodia, emerged in view of the vast amount of deadly land mines still hidden in the soil of the country.

As far as Cambodia's foreign policy is concerned, a special agreement committed the country "to maintain, preserve, and defend its sovereignty, independence, territorial integrity and inviolability, neutrality and national unity; the perpetual neutrality of Cambodia shall be proclaimed and enshrined in the Cambodian constitution, to be adopted after free and fair elections. The perpetual neutrality of Cambodia shall be proclaimed and enshrined in the Cambodian constitution, to be adopted after free and fair elections. Cambodia was therefore obligated to terminate treaties and agreements that are incompatible with its sovereignty [...] neutrality and national unity."

To translate those lofty objectives into practice proved to be far more difficult than to draft them. The low level of development required new demographic and geographic analyses. The reorganization of the civil police and general civil administration was hampered by the fact that the available manpower was composed of persons who were party functionaries without any useful training in public administration. UNTAC theoretically had the right to issue binding directives for all civil service offices and even to demand the dismissal of incapable civil servants. UNTAC'S force for reforming the civil service sector of the Cambodian administration was composed of 200 foreign and 600 local officials. UNTAC maintained in in each of Cambodia's 21 provinces headquarters, consisting of one Director, his Deputy, a Finance Officer and one Human Rights Officer.

Commanding and administering military units from so many different states proved to be another difficult task. UNTAC's military force had a strength of 15,900 men only. In addition there were 485 foreign military observers. A Mine Clearance Training Unit was to train thousands of Cambodians in the dangerous but urgently needed technique of clearing land mines. Internationally Cambodia had (and has) the world's highest percentage of persons mutilated by land mines. One platoon of 30 soldiers can clear no more than between 500 and 1.000s square meters a day.

Even after UNTAC's Mission had started, fighting continued in the centrally located province Kompong Thom, where the Khmer Rouge attempted to conquer certain villages and get control of certain national roads.

THE DECISIVE ELECTIONS

The general elections began on May 23rd, 1993 and could be conducted in a comparatively peaceful manner. The results were announced by the chief of the transitional administration. According to it there had been 4.011.631 valid votes:

> 1.824.188 votes (or 45.47 %) for Sihanouk's FUNCINPEC;
> 1.533.471 votes (38.23 %) for Hun Sen's Cambodian People's Party;
> 152.000.764 votes (3,8 %) for Son Sann's Buddhist Liberal Party.

The Red Khmer had refused to participate in the elections.

On September 24th, 1993 Prince Sihanouk, after taking an oath on the new constitution, was crowned Kind of Cambodia and assumed the positions of Cambodia's head of state and supreme commander of the armed forces. He then appointed both - his son Ranariddh and Hun Sen Prime - as Prime Ministers, with Ranariddh being in charge of the Ministries of Defense and of the Interior, while Hun Sen headed the Ministry of Public Security. Members of FUNCINPEC were put in charge of ten further ministries, while twelve Ministries went to Hun Sen's Cambodian People's Party, three Ministries to Son Sann's Buddhist Liberal Party and one ministry to the Moulinaka Party.

On September 24th, 1993 Norodom Sihanouk was crowned as King of Cambodia. At that occasion, he received a remarkable message from Red Khmer leader Khieu Samphan which reads in part:

"Your Respected Highness, on the solemn occasion of your ascension to the throne - as King - you will be respected and loved by the Cambodian nation and people, because you have dedicated your whole life [...] over half a century to defending the independence, sovereignty and territorial integrity of the Royal Kingdom of Cambodia - all of us in the Party of Democratic Kampuchea (Red Khmer) would like permission to join the entire Cambodian nation and people in expressing our most intense joy at this solemn historic political event. [...] May you enjoy Lord Buddha's five blessings! [...] Your Royal Highness, please forgive us for any inconvenience.! (This "inconvenience" included having tortured to death several of Sihanouk's children and other relatives.)

The general and tragic background of Cambodia's existence since the American Vietnam War was very well expressed by Henry A. Kissinger when he wrote in 1982:

No country has endured such a succession of miseries as Cambodia in the last decade, invaded and partially occupied by its North Vietnamese enemy in 1965, bombed by America after 1969, devastated by civil war, whose victors practiced genocide on their own compatriots, re-invaded by North Vietnam in 1978, and racked yet again by guerilla warfare, it has not enjoyed either peace nor order for nearly two decades.

DETERMINING FACTORS of SUCCESS

Asking why the unification of Cambodia has succeeded, one might construct a constellation (or configuration) containing the co-determinants of this difficult but successful operation. One key factor has been China's abandonment of its alliance with Vietnam and Peking's support for Cambodia's resistance against Hanoi's hegemonism on the Indochinese peninsula. A second major factor of almost equal significance was Moscow's decision also to cut its aid for Vietnam as one of the conditions for Moscow's rapprochement with Peking. Under those conditions, ASEAN, especially Indonesia and its Foreign Minister Ali Alitas, felt that their countries might play a constructive role, designed to limit the big power influence in Southeast Asia.

The United States was interested in the reduction of Soviet influence in a strategically most important region of Southeast Asia. Besides, in the early nineties Washington and Peking were about to reestablish their relations that had sharply worsened as one of the consequences of China's Tien An Men massacre. The participation of France was influenced by its former role as colonial power in Indochina, and last not least, there was the profound personal charisma of Prince Sihanouk and his almost legendary flexibility in seeking and balancing contacts with practically each of the powers involved in the interaction process of Cambodia's reunification. The unification process simultaneously brought democratization, at least of the forms of public life, although it must be said that the real structure of Cambodia's government since 2008 corresponds more to that of a conventional dictatorship. Marxism in Cambodia perished more openly than in China.

Favored by the rare occurrence of the fact that no power actively opposed the envisaged Cambodian reintegration process, the United Nations was able to perform, with success, its largest and most expensive overseas operations.

Describing the multi-dimensional efforts aiming at and bringing about Cambodia's reunification is not enough. There remains the question w h y those efforts have succeeded in the end. In order to gain meaningful answers to this question, it might be useful, as was said before, to construct a constellation or configuration analysis of those interacting factors that produced the desired objective. A historical background of international significance has been the defeat of the United States at the end of its ten years war in Indochina, going hand in hand with the seizure of power by Communist parties in the three states of Indochina, Vietnam, Laos and Cambodia. Those events greatly changed the geostrategic situation in Southeast Asia along one of the world's most important shipping routes. But subsequent events did not confirm the formerly influential American "Domino Theory", claiming that a Communist victory in one country would lead to series of follow up aggressions and expansion in other countries. Instead, there developed a sharp conflict between Cambodia and Vietnam, resulting in part from territorial disputes as well as from Cambodia's fierce resistance to Vietnam's hegemonic imperialism that had sought in vain to unite the three Indochinese states under the leadership of Hanoi.

At the end of 1978, Vietnam began a large seize military offensive against the Red Khmer who ruled Cambodia, leading to the conquest of about two thirds of the territory of that country. Hanoi declared its intention of nevertheless integrating the states of Indochina under its leadership. On January 11, 1979 Cambodian Communists opposed the Red Khmer, but cooperating with Vietnam proclaimed in Phnom Penh a People's Republic of Cambodia. Internationally this new regime was recognized only by the Soviet Union and its East European satellites. China, which in December 1978 had obtained diplomatic relations with the United States at Peking's own conditions, started two months later a military "punitive campaign" against Vietnam, but had to withdraw its forces after only 27 days. On the other side, Deng Xiaoping in January and February 1979 had paid a highly successful visit to the United States. In spite of serious disagreements caused by American reactions to China's Tien An Men massacre, America's China policy basically remained on the course that had been started by Nixon and Kissinger. As already mentioned, the Soviet Union also ended its cold war with China by imposing on it three conditions, including Moscow's termination of its support for Vietnam.

Thus big power politics around Indochina had developed in such a way that none of the major powers entertained any interest in creating a new crisis situation. While China's limited war against Vietnam had been a failure, Moscow's cessation of major aid for Vietnam, as demanded by Peking, became a key factor in changing the situation in Indochina. In addition, most Western nations and Japan had imposed trade embargoes upon Vietnam. Vietnam withdrew from Cambodia, ended its hegemonic policies in Indochina, and showed its readiness to participate in a negotiated settlement of the Cambodian issue. Vietnam nevertheless could gain some comfort from the fact that most of Cambodia was under the control of the pro-Vietnamese People's Republic of Cambodia where Hun Sen and Heng Samrim had become the leading political figures. The main loser of the developments of the 1970ies and 1980ies had been the Red Khmer. But they temporarily continued to exist as relatively strongest force within the tripartite Cambodian resistance government, residing in border areas of Cambodia, headed by Prince Sihanouk, and recognized by the majority of foreign states as the legitimate government of Cambodia. It called itself "Coalition Government of Democratic Kampuchea".

The United States, in the words of its Secretary of State James Baker, in July 1988 had however performed "a complete U-turn" of its Indochina policy by seeking to establish an open dialog with Vietnam and Cambodia. Of even greater impact was a rare joint statement by the five permanent members of the U.N. Security Council of January 1990, anticipating all the major elements of the "Final Act of the Paris Conference on Cambodia" signed in Paris October 23 1991. And indeed all of the five veto powers of the U.N. had reasons of their own for opposing Vietnamese hegemony in Indochina. The USA and France had both suffered from having been defeated by Vietnam after frustrating years of war. China having been nearly defeated by Vietnam, opposed the idea of a Vietnam-dominated Indochina and wanted to punish Vietnam for the expulsion of hundreds of thousands of ethnic Chinese, formerly residing in Vietnam. Impressed by the dramatic collapse of Communism in Russia, Germany, and Eastern Europe, Hun Sen's Cambodian People's Party disavowed Communism as their official ideology and claimed, at least, to have accepted multi-party democracy and market economy. The Red Khmer were at least formally integrated into Sihanou's tripartite resistance government. They insisted that their crimes should not be mentioned in any official document of Cambodia's national reintegration process. One therefore spoke of those crimes only euphemistically as "evil practices of the past". The ASEAN states, most actively represented by Indonesia, were strongly interested in removing conditions of tension and crisis from Southeast Asia. On November 14-th 1991 Prince Sihanouk triumphantly returned to Cambodia and ten days later the Khmer Rouge obtained a representative office in Phnom Penh, while in January of 1992 America's trade embargo against Cambodia was lifted.

All in all, the reunification of Cambodia emerged stage by stage and event by event as the result of multinational, bilateral, and individual efforts of Western and Asian-Pacific nations. With UNTAC, the United Nations Transitional Authority in Cambodia - the UN provided the legitimized organizational structure and instrument for inspiring, supervising and organizing Cambodia's renewal, re-unification and reconstruction efforts, in line with the so called Agreements on the Comprehensive Political Settlement of the Cambodia Conflict, signed in Paris October 23 1991. UNTAC's most difficult task and achievement was the institutionalization of cooperation between parties and governments that shortly before still have been enemies, being at war with each other.

The process of Cambodian reunification was perceptibly influenced by the fact that it occurred in an era of great changes in world politics, characterized by the disintegration of the Soviet Union and her satellite empire, by the re-unification of Germany, by the end of the Cold War and the dynamic growth of Chinese power. The normalization of conditions and regional power relations in Indochina thus corresponded well with the historical trend of time in the early 1990ies.

SELECTED LITERATURE

Akashi, Yasushi: The Challenge of Peacekeeping in Cambodia, in: International Peacekeeping, Vol. 1, No 2, Summer 1994, pp. 204-215 (Akashi was Chairman of UNTAC).

Armstrong, John (ed.): Sihanouk Speaks, Walker and Co. New York 1964.

Chandler, David : A History of Cambodia, Boulder, Colorado 1992.

Doyle, Michael W. and Suuntharalingam, N.: The U.N. in Cambodia. Lessons for Complex Peace-keeping, in: International Peacekeeping Vol. 1, No. 2, Summer 1994, pp 117-147.

Hazdra, Peter: Die UNO Friedensoperation in Kambodscha, Peter Lang, Frankfurt a. M. 1997

Jennar, Roul: After the UNTAC MISSION. Christian Conference of Asia, Kiernan, Ben ed.: Genocide and Democracy in Cambodia, New Haven CT 1993.

Kindermann, G.K. / Meyer-Lindenberg: Indochina. Krisenherd der Weltpolitik, München 1981.

Löschmann, Heike: Die Friedensidee des kambodschanischen Buddhismus, in: Die Friedensidee des kambodschanischen Buddhismus. In: Südostasien Informationen 1/1992.

Muscat, Robert J.: Rebuilding Cambodia. Problems of Governance and Human Resources

Raszelenberg, P. u. Schier, P.: The Cambodia Conflict. Search for a Settlement 1979-1991. An Analytical Chronology, Hamburg 1995.

Ross, Robert: China and the Cambodian Peace Process, in: Asian Survey Vol. XXXI, No. 12 Dec. 1991, pp. 1170-1185.

Schier, Peter: Die UN Friedensmission und die Wahlen in Kambodscha, in: Südostasien aktuell, July 1993.

Human Rights Watch / Asia: Cambodia at War, New York 1995

Sihanouk, Norodom / Bernard Krisher: Sihanouk's Erinnerungen an Staatsmänner und Herrscher, Bangkok 1990.

IV)

Power Shifts in Europe in the Wake of the Current Financial Crisis. Political and Economic Analyses

Political Power Shifts in Europe as Result of the Economic and Financial Crisis in Europe

Harald Bergbauer

The elections to the European Parliament in May 2014 implied two major surprises: first the rise of voters from 43 percent in 2009 to now 49 percent, an increase that seems to testify a higher interest in the European Union in 2014 than five years before, and second the rise of right and left wing parties.[1] The United Kingdom Independence Party (UKIP) got with almost 27 percent of the vote the highest approval of all British parties, the French Front National (FN) got 25 percent of the vote, and in Germany the Eurosceptic "Alternative for Germany" (AFD), founded only in 2013, obtained at its first election to the European Parliament already 7 percent. Many other parties in smaller European countries like the anti-immigrant Danish People's Party or the Hungarian far-right Jobbik could be mentioned to underline the strength of right wing, left wing, and especially, anti-European parties. Skepticism regarding the European Union and the Euro was, according to many interpretations, the main winner of the election.[2]

Asking for the reasons to explain this Eurosceptic turn in the history of the European Union, one is quickly referred to 1. the currently dominant position of Germany within the EU, 2. the currency union which is undermining the confidence to the EU, and 3. the lack of democracy which means a threat for the rule of law in Europe and which entails the powerful bureaucratic apparatus in Brussels that goes hand in hand with a shortage of power in the single member states. These features of the European

---

1 A helpful illustration of the European Parliament Elections and its outcome is available at: http://graphics.wsj.com/european-elections-2014 (retrieved April 21, 2015). The authors hint at the fact that Eurosceptic and anti-European Union parties made big gains in the first European elections since the euro-zone debt crisis has shaken the continent.

2 Cfr. Higgins, Andrew: Populists' Rise in Europe Vote Shakes Leaders, in: International New York Times, May 26, 2014, online at: http://www.nytimes.com/2014/05/27/world/europe/established-parties-rocked-by-anti-europe-vote.html (retrieved April 21, 2015).

Union arouse power shifts in the European Union which will alter its current constellation.

I) Germany's Predominance in the EU and its Consequences

In September 2013 the British magazine "The Economist", also famous for its penetrative and often funny illustrations, put a telling picture on its cover page: It shows the German chancellor, Angela Merkel, standing right in the center of a landscape and being surrounded by eminent national symbols of some leading European states like the Eiffel Tower of Paris, the Leaning Tower of Pisa, the Parthenon of the Acropolis, or the Big Ben of London. But while all the buildings shown are in a state of break-up or disrepair, Mrs. Merkel stands upright in the middle, in a firm position and seemingly not much worried about what is going on in her immediate environment. She alone stands on a solid (Greek!) column and enjoys the sun – exclusively – shining on her.

Looking back to the origins and the evolution of the EU, its erstwhile founders and concurrent shapers had a completely different model in mind than the predominance of one particular country. The original idea after WW II was to overcome than rampant nationalism and to create a peaceful continent by fostering economic cooperation. And the best way to defeat nationalism was by launching cooperation between the dominant powers, especially between France and Germany. The success of the six founding countries (France, Germany, Italy; Belgium, Netherlands, Luxemburg) has led to the first enlargement in 1973, when the United Kingdom, Ireland and Denmark joined the European Community. This "Northern enlargement" was counterbalanced by a "Southern enlargement", in the course of which first Greece (1981) and then Spain and Portugal (both in 1986) became members of the Union. The next enlargement came about with the admission of Austria, Finland, and Sweden in 1995, few years after the collapse of the Soviet Union and its satellite states. At this time almost the whole of Western Europe was rallied under the protecting roof of the European Union. The biggest single enlargement in terms of people and number of countries happened in 2004, already more than one decade ago, when ten former Communist countries joined the EU (Czech Republic, Estonia, Cyprus, Latvia, Lithuania, Hungary, Malta, Poland, Slovakia, and

Slovenia). The project of expanding the Union came to a provisional end with the access of Romania and Bulgaria in 2007 and Croatia in 2013.[3]

(Source: The Economist, Sept. 14-20, 2013)

The outcome is a (to a huge extent artificial) entity which today consists of 28 member states; most of them have completely different historic traditions and political cultures. People in the Northern countries differ in many respects (attitude to work, productivity, frugality, lifestyle, etc.) from those living in the European South, and those of the former Eastern countries were raised and trained under political regimes which contradicted consciously the value systems prevalent in the West. The conflict between the capitalistic and democratic countries in the West and the Communist and autocratic regimes in the East came to an official end in 1989/90 on the level of political orders and institutions. The value systems of the people, however, could not so easily be overcome and are, in part, still present to-

---

3 Very instructive political analyses of the history of the European Union have been edited by Desmond Dinan (ed.): Origins and Evolution of the European Union, 2. edition, Oxford 2014. A more historical (and internationally much praised) approach was published by the eminent scientist Tony Judt: Postwar. A History of Europe since 1945, London 2010.

day, one generation after the collapse of Communism. This can be felt also today. It's needless to say that the various enlargements contain deep challenges for the cohesion of the Union. The problem is obvious: The bigger institutions become, the more difficult it is to find common bases for compromise and consensus. An entity encompassing 28 countries instead of 6 contains a huge potential of conflict, and it is indeed arduous to reach to stable agreements, as negotiations on the European level demonstrate as soon as serious political issues are at stake.

For decades the outstanding feature of the European Union was the so called Franco-German axis. Common incentives and proposals of these two countries had the best chances of being accepted by the other members. Since some years, however, the economic and political power of Germany is undermining this axis. Germany became stronger, especially in economic terms, and France weaker. Germany developed from the "sick man of Europe" to its economically dominant power, whereas France's national economy deteriorated during the last years.[4] The erstwhile axis of the EU is beginning to dissolve or even break up. New political coalitions between countries are being forged; a new pattern of the EU is evolving.

II) The Currency Union and the Loss of Confidence

The European Union today consists of 28 member states. The currency union, however, comprises currently only 19 members. Nine members of the EU refuse to be or to become a member of the currency union. Its actual members are all but equal with respect to their economic performance. These 18 states differ profoundly with regard to economic power, and they have usually deviant, sometimes contradictory administrative, tax and social systems, and the rules directing their labor markets display great differences, too. Did the creators of the currency union ignore these differences, or did they simply neglect them by thinking these concerns will be overcome sooner or later?

---

4 This far-reaching change is analyzed by Dustmann, Christian / Fitzenberger, Bernd / Schönberg, Uta, and Spitz-Oener, Alexandra: From Sick Man of Europe to Economic Superstar: Germany's Resurgent Economy, in: Journal of Economic Perspectives 28 (1), 2014, 167-188.

Political scientists and historians today know that the member states joining the currency union in 1999 (the Euro itself was introduced on that basis only in January 2002) had different motives to do so: In France the single currency was seen as a way of getting rid of the enormous strong German Mark as the European lead currency and as a means of confining the hegemony of the German Federal Bank. Southern European countries like Italy or Greece thought that the creation of a European single currency could go hand in hand with the adoption of the German model of monetary policy and the importation of the German economic success. Even in Germany some people were optimistic about the creation of the single currency expecting the euro to become weaker than the German Mark, thereby alleviating the sale of German commodities abroad.[5]

All countries joining the currency union acted on the assumption that the different degrees of economic efficiency could be counterbalanced in the course of time. This assumption of reaching an adjustment between countries with wholly different economic performances was often called the "birth defect" of the current economic problems. How did the advocates of that decision justify this incisive measure, what arguments were brought forward for such a deliberation which has no successful historical specimen? The advocates of the currency union maintained that on the basis of a currency union the member states and their economies would start an ever closer cooperation which, in the end, would lead to the desired political union. This position was called "cornerstone theory", because the currency union was considered to be the cornerstone or basis for an ensuing political cooperation. If the economic exchange between the European member states worked, then the political cooperation would naturally follow suit. The opponents of this position held that without a working political union a currency union will never work. A currency union can only be thought of as a kind of consequence of an established political union. If the member states of the European Union worked more and more closely together, the economic cooperation would automatically ensue. Its propo-

---

5 See the excellent account of the different motives of the 11 European member states which in 1999 started the single currency and the Economic and Monetary Union, by Andrew Moravcsik: Europe after the Crisis, in: Foreign Affairs 91, May/June 2012, pp. 54-68. Worth reading is also the more economic analysis of the European Monetary Union by Qin Wang on: A Macroeconomic Assessment of the European Monetary Union, online at: http://aei.pitt.edu/29778/1/WangMacroeconAssessmEU ediEUMA.pdf (retrieved April 23, 2015).

nents called it therefore the "coronation theory". The political protagonists of this debate can easily be identified and named: France argued primarily in favor of the so called "cornerstone theory", the German Federal Bank and a majority of Germans were convinced that only the "coronation theory" be correct.[6]

The current economic turmoil in Europe has its roots less in the housing crisis, set out in the US in 2008, than rather in the currency union. In the years before 1999 each country in Europe could steer its economic performance by manipulating its exchange rate. The currency union excludes this option. The exchange rates of the countries participating in the currency union are fixed. The important measure of altering and adjusting the exchange rate to the economic performance of a given country was abandoned with the start of the currency union. Regarding the current (economic and political) turbulences in the EU, politicians look for ways to alleviate the effects of fixed exchange rates. There are four options: 1. the reduction of real wages, 2. the mobility of the labor force, 3. transfer payments, und 4. the limitation of free trade. I briefly enter all four areas.

1. The competitiveness of a country can be restored (or improved) by reducing the real wages. This, however, did not happen in the debt-ridden countries in the last decade. On the contrary: Economic institutes furnish evidence that between 2000 and 2008 Romania and Latvia had with 331,7 respectively 188.5% the highest increase in wages, Greece had with 39.6% and Ireland with 30.3% a high increase the same period, whereas Germany had with a minus of 0.8% the least increase in real wages in the whole Euro zone.[7]

---

6 See the balanced and knowledgeable assessment of Hubert Zimmermann on the various points of view in discussion: The Euro under Scrutiny: Histories and Theories of European Monetary Integration, in: Contemporary European History 10 (2), 2001, pp. 333-341.

7 Cf. the German Statistics website, on:
   http://www.eu-info.de/deutsche-europapolitik/umfragen-statistiken-deutschland/rea llohn (retrieved on April 25, 2015).

Romania 331,7	Finland 18,9
Latvia 188,5	Sweden 17,9
Estonia 132,5	Cyprus 12,8
Lithuania 104,4	Netherlands 12,4
Hungary 66,7	France 9,6
Bulgaria 51,9	Luxembourg 8,1
Czech Republic 49,1	Malta 7,9
Slovakia 48,1	Italy 7,5
Slovenia 40,3	Belgium 7,2
Greece 39,6	Spain 4,6
Ireland 30,3	Portugal 3,3
Great Britain 26,1	Austria 2,9
Denmark 19,0	Germany -0,8
Poland 19,0	

Source: Eu-Info.de (German source)

2. Economic imbalances can be tackled by mobilizing the labor force. People in economically weak or underdeveloped regions could move to regions or countries with high employment rates. Indeed, since some years people from Spain, Portugal, Greece, Italy and other countries move to Germany to find jobs. Given the linguistic barriers and cultural differences in Europe, the labor mobility is and remains rather restricted in Europe.

3. A third possibility of minimizing or even equalizing economic imbalances is capital transfer from one country to another. Such transfers do exist within some nation states, for example in Germany in the shape of the so called "financial equalization". According to the German federal constitution the richer states have to support the poorer ones by transferring equalization payments to them.[8] This idea of capital transfer between different national entities has been transmitted from the national level to the

---

8 Cf. Article 107 II of the German Constitution: The law "shall ensure a reasonable equalization of the disparate financial capacities of the Lander, with due regard for the financial capacities and needs of municipalities (associations of municipalities)". This provision is object of much quarrel in Germany, for obvious reasons: the rich German states don't want to transfer their money to the poorer states, because (first) it has been earned by the citizens of a particular state and should therefore also be spent for them, and (second) because the donor countries argue that if they just transfer parts of their budget to poorer German states then these don't have an incentive to work and trade more efficiently in economic terms. If the transfers rouse much trouble within one (rather wealthy) nation state, how much more trouble is caused within a multitude of wholly different national states, as in the EU?

European level. The judgments about the use of this instrument are well known in Europe: The citizens of the donor countries criticize that their hard-earned money is given away to bail-out foreign countries, where these rescuing activities are not even appreciated, and the citizens of the recipient countries criticize that the (often too small) amounts of money are bound to measures of structural reform which they often decline and reject. The European Union is currently on the way to becoming a kind of "transfer union", because some member states seem to be able to survive only on the basis of huge rescue funds.[9] At present, in the middle of 2015, the protests of both the donors and the receivers are rather strong in Europe, and obviously not appropriate for strengthening the European Union.

4. The fourth and last alternative to fixed exchange rates consists in the limitation of free trade. Economically strong countries could voluntarily restrict their exports, European (and non-European) goods could be liable to customs duty, or certain product licenses could limit the sale of goods into the EU or the trade within it.[10] It is beyond question that this option contradicts the endeavors of most countries in the world to abolish trade barriers in order to augment the general wealth.

The aim of the currency union was to prepare a solid basis for the political union. The countries of Europe should close ranks, intensify their cooperation, and thereby increase their wealth. A peaceful and powerful Europe as one block in the midst of a world of six or seven other major power blocks is the leading idea for Europe since the end of the Cold War.[11] So far this goal has not been reached: hard controversies on various eco-

---

9　The "Deutsche Bank Research" hints in its paper "EU Monitor 81. Reports on European Integration" from August 2, 2011 already to the different dimensions of a transfer union. The paper analyses not only the economic implications, but the political consequences as well, pointing to the "political tensions" these transfers could fuel. Online at: https://www.dbresearch.com/PROD/DBR_INTERNET_EN-PROD/PROD0000000000276427/A+European+transfer+union%3A+How+large, +how+powerful.PDF. The literature on the topic of the European Monetary Union as a potential transfer union is gargantuan and needs no further (current) indications or references.

10　See for the whole issue the arguments of Dominik Geppert in his (German) book on "Ein Europa, das es nicht gibt. Die fatale Sprengkraft des Euro" (Engl.: A Europe that does not exist. The Fatal Blasting Power of the Euro), Berlin et al., 2013, especially pp. 76-82.

11　See the account of Henry Kissinger in his study on "Diplomacy" which was published in 1994 and tackles the new world order which developed after the collapse of Communism. He enumerates as major players on the international scene six

nomic, political and personal issues as well as serious interest conflicts made the relationships between the member states of the European Union rather worse than better. Germany is blamed for not doing enough to endorse the weak national economies of the Euro zone, and many Germans themselves scold other European people's governments and citizens of not implementing necessary structural reforms in their countries. The result today is not closer cooperation, but rather distance and estrangement in Europe. The assumption seems likely that some member states, especially the strong ones, would be better off if they had never joined the currency union. A feeling of dissatisfaction is spreading across Europe, at least in view of the current shape of the EU.

This outcome could have been expected from the very beginning of the European Monetary Union: the different countries in the European Union have different levels of economic performance. The countries of the EU differ profoundly regarding productivity, public spending ratio, fiscal discipline, education of their population, extension of infrastructure, pension obligations, etc. These factors are the reason for different exchange rates and prohibit, on principle, a uniform monetary policy. Leading economists wanted to impede the implementation of the Euro (but not the further development of the EU), but politicians knew better.[12]

III) The Danger to the Rule of Law

The economic crisis is only one aspect of the current situation in Europe, even if it is the most striking one. Probably more important is the challenge to the rule of law on the basis of decisions made by the European Union. An outstanding example is the provision in article 125 of the "Treaty on the Functioning of the European Union" which states:

---

major powers, namely the United States, Europe, China, Japan, Russia, and possibly India (Diplomacy, New York et al. 1994, p. 23).

12 Very interesting in this regard is the study on "The euro: It can't happen. It's a bad idea. It won't last. US economists on the EMU 1989-2002", written by Lars Jonung and Eoin Drea, edited by the European Commission, Economic Paper 395, December 2009. The authors give a survey of about 170 publications by US economists evidencing the widespread skepticism about the monetary union in leading circles of the US. Online at: http://ec.europa.eu/economy_finance/publicati ons/publication16345_en.pdf (accessed June 24, 2015).

"The Union shall not be liable for or assume the commitments of central governments, regional, local or other public authorities, other bodies governed by public law, or public undertakings of any Member State." And: "A Member State shall not be liable for or assume the commitments of central governments, regional, local or other public authorities, other bodies governed by public law, or public undertakings of another Member State."

The liability exclusion, clearly articulated in this important legal document, has been sidestepped by high European officials in the past and is being bypassed also in our present. The best example is given by the current president of the European Central Bank, Mario Draghi, who declared officially in a speech at the Global Investment Conference in London on July 26, 2012 that "the ECB is ready to do whatever it takes to preserve the euro"[13]. The intention "to do whatever it takes" on part of the ECB is outright contradicting the legal provision in art. 125 I of the above mentioned treaty. Other examples for a breach of the law could be added: The ECB offered European banks great amounts of liquidity since 2010, it implemented comprehensive bailout programs to crisis-ridden countries such as Greece, Ireland, Spain, and Portugal, and set up monstrous debt instruments like the "European Financial Stability Facility" (EFSF)[14] or the "European Stability Mechanism" (ESM)[15]. So far the last measure to support (or rescue?) the European Monetary Union's policy is the European Central Bank's program to monthly purchase bonds to the amount of 60 billion Euros between March 2015 and September 2016.[16]

It seems as if the proverb "Necessity knows no law" would be part of the European policy. In Germany the "priority of the juridical over the political" constitutes a firm principle of all variants of politics, but it seems

---

13 Speech by Mario Draghi at the Global Investment Conference in London, July 26, 2012, online, for instance, at: www.ecb.europa.eu/press/key/date/2012/html/sp120 726.en.html (accessed on June 30, 2014). The whole sentence from which these words are taken reads: "Within our mandate, the ECB is ready to do whatever it takes to preserve the euro. And believe me, it will be enough." Immediately after this statement the question was raised whether the ECB will actually remain within its mandate or transgress it for rescuing the euro.

14 Official information about the (temporary) EFSF – "European Financial Stability Facility" is to be found online at http://www.efsf.europa.eu/about/index.htm.

15 Official information and current news on the (permanent) ESM – "European Stability Mechanism" is online at http://www.esm.europa.eu.

16 Reliable details and explanations of this "asset purchase programme" are online at the ECB's website: https://www.ecb.europa.eu/mopo/implement/omt/html/index.e n.html (retrieved: June 25, 2015).

that in other European countries the position of the law is handled much more flexible. If political "necessities" prevail, the economy and the law have to be adjusted. What explanation exists for this difference in the political culture of some European countries? Probably the fact that in Germany the rule of law is much older than democracy and that it is therefore in highest esteem; in Italy and France, however, where the idea of the "priority of the political over the juridical" seems to prevail, it is not excluded at all that the judiciary is allowed to pursue certain political tasks, at least from time to time and (only) in emergency cases.

The decisions of the European Commission in Brussels seem also to be determined by political criteria rather than by legal ones. European politics is increasingly influencing domestic politics of their member states, thereby frequently dominating and even overruling national decisions. The budget law may serve as one instance: in Greece, Portugal, Ireland, and Cyprus representatives of Brussels interfere in national affairs by making decisions regarding their budget law. And the budget law is the most prominent law of any parliament. Some hundred years of parliamentary history are menaced by the measures of the European Union to rescue the euro. Recent developments of the EU show that the basic legal principle "pacta sunt servanda" (agreements must be kept) has lost its compelling character, and that bailout measures initiated by the EU are undermining the eminent importance of national parliaments. The decisions of the European Commission seem to be more important than those of single national governments, and national governments sometimes make decisions in view of future deliberations from the European Commission to avoid contradictions and political tensions.

IV) Power Shifts of the European Union

So far this account argued that the EU is currently characterized by a certain economic and political hegemony of Germany which did not only stir up sympathies in Europe (I), it emphasized that the introduction of the currency union in 1999 led to difficulties we are still struggling with today (II), and it strove to make clear that the efforts to rescue the currency union and the project of the European union as a whole led to decisions which violate valid European law (III). The topic of the EU's foreign relations towards other states has not been touched upon. Given its inner heterogeneity and the endeavors of some of its members to determine the international relations of the whole community it is evident that the EU is far from implementing something like a common foreign and security policy. The civil war in Yugoslavia in the middle of the 1990s revealed similar interest conflicts and diverging positions of the EU's member states than the American war against Iraq in 2003 or the international military deployments in Syria since 2011. The European Union as community is no real political actor in international politics, but it is the single European member states like France, Great Britain, and Germany that determine the "European" foreign-policy agenda. Unfortunately in many cases the foreign policies even of these three countries differ from each other.

Scientists and politicians alike often discuss the final end of the European Union. Where shall this historically and internationally unique project finally lead to? Three options stand out in public debates: 1. The "United States of Europe", usually discussed under the heading "political union", the essence of which would consist in the creation of central institutions to coordinate the economic and fiscal policies. 2. The advancement of the EU towards a genuine "transfer and liability union" which would entail a common liability for all debts in Europe and the introduction of euro bonds the German chancellor (and the majority of the German population) so far strictly rejects. 3. An alternative to these two scenarios would be the idea of integration by way of decentralization and enhanced competition. The economic and fiscal policies of the single member states should be coordinated better than hitherto and the community would insist that each country reorganizes its budget and implements the necessary structural reforms to be or to become a really competitive member. Single coordinative and supportive measures from the EU would be part of this perspective.

The European Union at present is not on the way to closer cooperation or better harmonization. The contrary holds true. The Union today is split in an at least twofold way: 19 of the 28 member states of the EU are part of the euro zone, and 9 are not. The participants in the euro zone are again split in debtor countries and creditor countries, and the difference between them is in part enormous. The currency concept was devised to improve solidity and solidarity in Europe, it caused, however, quarrel and cleavage. The quality of the Franco-German axis is deteriorating; France and Germany are seeking for new ways of cooperating and leading the EU project. But currently we observe different trends: France intensifies its relations with Italy and other South European countries to boost its (and their) interests, which more and more deviate from those of her German neighbor;

whereas Germany orients itself increasingly toward Poland[17] and Great Britain. Poland is the most successful country of the former Communist states; its economy grew more than that of any other countries in the EU since the collapse of Communism, and it has cordial relations with both Germany and Russia. Poland implemented deep structural reforms since 1990, thereby pleasantly setting itself apart from some Southern European members that refuse to do so.[18] And Britain, although highly anti-European, incorporates those values that are vital for the German chancellor: it has a successful liberal market economy, fosters competition, and incorporates the important idea of self-responsibility. As events in 2014 showed, when the European Counsel was looking for the president of the European Commission, and Mr. Cameron threatened the exit of Great Britain from the EU, Ms Merkel emphatically pursued the goal of keeping Britain in the EU; she said that Britain is "a vital counterweight to France and the southern countries in keeping the EU liberal and pushing for freer trade, less regulation and tighter budgeting"[19].

The conclusion is almost obvious: The EU project, originally aimed at bringing its members closer together, caused many conflicts and cleavages in the last years. Metamorphoses and signs of disintegration of formerly stable relations became visible. Whether the originating new partnerships and alliances in Europe may be able to replace the old relationships and patterns, nobody knows.

---

17 See the instructive article on "Leaving the West Behind. Germany looks East" by Hans Kundnani who shows in detail how Germany's attitude toward the West has changed in the last years, in: Foreign Affairs, vol. 94, no. 1, Jan./Febr. 2015, pp. 108-116.

18 See "Poland's second golden age: Europe's unlikely star", in: The Economist, No. 26, June 28, 2014, p. 13 and the "Special Report on Poland" in the same issue. An economic account of Poland's spectacular economic development has been published by Hartmut Lehman under the title "The Polish Growth Miracle: Outcome of Persistent Reform Efforts", online at: http://ftp.iza.org/pp40.pdf (retrieved April 22, 2015). Lehmann states that the radical break immediately after the fall of Communism and its consistent orientation towards the Western market economy constitute the main reason for Poland's economic success.

19 Germany and the EU. Still a sorry mess, in: The Economist, No. 26, June 28, 2014, p. 23.

V) Current and future power constellations in the EU

The collapse of the Soviet Union in 1990 signified the end of the bipolar world which characterized, in various guises, the history of the short 20th century. The consequence of the break-up of the old order was the emergence of a "New World Order" (George Bush) whose eminent feature was the multipolarity of few major political and economic powers. Henry Kissinger compared the newly emerged order to the pattern of the European states' system of the 18th and 19th century; both are marked by competition and rivalry of a number of important states. The new world order would develop similarly to the old European order, but it would stretch across the whole globe; as major players on the international scene he mentioned the USA, Europe, China, Japan, Russia, and (probably) India.[20]

A quarter of a century after the decline of Communism we can confirm the multipolarity of international politics and judge the development each of the powers mentioned went through. In the case of the European Union there are first and foremost the great enlargements of 1995, 2004 and 2007, but there is also the introduction of the European Monetary Union since 1999 and the current financial crisis in Greece. The common currency which was supposed to unify the European member states and strengthen their solidarity, caused, however, tensions and disruptions. The European project seems to be in danger. This is problematic for two reasons: first because Europe could become in general a weaker actor in the concert of the major powers, and second because Europe threatens to languish exactly in a situation in which the field of international politics is changing. According to many analyses the West, and here especially Europe, is losing power and influence which are moving toward the Asian continent. Niall Ferguson states in his treatise on "The Great Degeneration. How Institutions Decay and Economies Die" that in four areas the West is in decline: in the field of democracy, capitalism, the rule of law, and finally in the field of civil society. The West has less growth than the East and seems to enter a "state of standstill".[21] The German journalist Jan Roß puts the same situation more bluntly when he maintains that the center of the world is switching from West to East: into the Islamic violence-East,

---

20 Cfr. Kissinger, Henry: Die sechs Säulen der Weltordnung, Berlin 1992 [Engl.: The Six Pillars of World Order].
21 Cfr. Ferguson, Niall: The Great Degeneration. How Institutions Decay and Economies Die", London 2012.

into the Russian revenge-East, and finally into the Asian boom-East. The world is faced with a "loss of power and significance of the West" that will be especially challenging for the European Union. Europe has been for centuries the minority on top of a progressive movement, right now it seems to be a privileged class of yesterday which is sliding into the defensive. Europe is becoming a spectator in the face of the global power shift.[22]

There exists, of course, no general acceptance of statements like these. Even if most interpreters say that the European Union is currently in crisis, they point to ways out of it. A strengthened transatlantic partnership is mentioned in the same way like a division of the European member states in core and periphery members. Most important however is the successful handling of its current economic crisis which stirs up consequences far beyond the economic sphere. Regardless of the power shifts within the EU which will change - but not destroy - the European project, the European Union must regain its former strength and represent the values it has detected and developed over centuries, like basic human rights, freedom and equality, the rule of law, democracy, etc. in international affairs. Only by stressing these and other traditional strengths the European Union can remain also in the years to come a major political and economic actor on the international scene.

REFERENCES

Dinan, Desmond (ed.): Origins and Evolution of the European Union, 2. edition, Oxford 2014.

Draghi, Mario: Speech at the Global Investment Conference in London, July 26, 2012, online at: www.ecb.europa.eu/press/key/date/2012/html/sp120726.en.html

Dustmann, Christian / Fitzenberger, Bernd / Schönberg, Uta, and Spitz-Oener, Alexandra: From Sick Man of Europe to Economic Superstar: Germany's Resurgent Economy, in: Journal of Economic Perspectives 28 no. 1, 2014, 167-188.

EFSF – "European Financial Stability Facility", online at: http://www.efsf.europa.eu/a bout/index.htm.

ESM – "European Stability Mechanism", online at: http://www.esm.europa.eu.

---

22 Cfr. Roß, Jan: Was bleibt von uns? Das Ende der westlichen Weltherrschaft, Berlin 2008 [Engl.: What Remains of us? The End of Western World Dominance].

EU Monitor 81. Reports on European Integration, in: Deutsche Bank Research: https:// www.dbresearch.com/PROD/DBR_INTERNET_EN-PROD/PROD0000000000276 427/A+European+transfer+union%3A+How+large,+how+powerful.PDF

Ferguson, Niall: The Great Degeneration. How Institutions Decay and Economies Die, London 2012.

Geppert, Dominik: Ein Europa, das es nicht gibt. Die fatale Sprengkraft des Euro [Engl.: A Europe that does not exist. The Fatal Blasting Power of the Euro], Berlin et al., 2013.

Germany and the EU. Still a sorry mess, in: The Economist, no. 26, June 28, 2014, p. 23.

Higgins, Andrew: Populists' Rise in Europe Vote Shakes Leaders, in: International New York Times, May 26, 2014, online at: http://www.nytimes.com/2014/05/27/w orld/europe/established-parties-rocked-by-anti-europe-vote.html

Jonung, Lars / Drea, Eoin: The euro: It can't happen. It's a bad idea. It won't last. US economists on the EMU 1989-2002, ed. by the European Commission, Economic Paper 395, December 2009. Online at: http://ec.europa.eu/economy_finance/publica tions/publication16345_en.pdf.

Judt, Tony: Postwar. A History of Europe since 1945, London 2010.

Kissinger, Henry: Die sechs Säulen der Weltordnung, Berlin 1992 [Engl.: The Six Pillars of World Order].

Kissinger, Henry: Diplomacy, New York et al. 1994.

Kundnani, Hans: Leaving the West Behind. Germany looks East, in: Foreign Affairs, vol. 94, no. 1, Jan. / Febr. 2015, pp. 108-116.

Lehman, Hartmut: The Polish Growth Miracle: Outcome of Persistent Reform Efforts, online at: http://ftp.iza.org/pp40.pdf.

Moravcsik, Andrew: Europe after the Crisis, in: Foreign Affairs, vol. 91, May/June 2012, pp. 54-68.

Poland's second golden age: Europe's unlikely star, in: The Economist, no. 26, June 28, 2014, p. 13.

Roß, Jan: Was bleibt von uns? Das Ende der westlichen Weltherrschaft, Berlin 2008 [Engl.: What Remains of us? The End of Western World Dominance].

The Economist, Sept. 14-20, 2013.

Wang, Qin: A Macroeconomic Assessment of the European Monetary Union, online at: http://aei.pitt.edu/29778/1/WangMacroeconAssessmEUediEUMA.pdf

Zimmermann, Hubert: The Euro under Scrutiny: Histories and Theories of European Monetary Integration, in: Contemporary European History 10 (2), 2001, pp. 333-341.

The Political and Economic Effects of the Eastward Expansion of the European Union for Germany

Ralf Thomas Göllner

The caesura of 1990 created new dependencies and vulnerabilities leading to the necessity of a wider and at the same time deeper European integration. German power, after the Second World War a "long-standing implicit concern for European integration",[1] and decreasing constraints after the fall of the iron curtain as well as German unification, respectively, led to a new political environment in Europe. Contrary to the sometimes expressed concerns about rising German hegemony, unification's immediate aftermath was characterized by an even deeper co-operation between France and Germany and an emerging leadership of both countries pushing integration ahead. Together the two states were able to offer leadership to the European integration process. The Maastricht Treaty, signed on 7 February 1992, introduced important changes notably in widening the scope of integration and marked "a new stage in the process of creating an ever closer union among the peoples of Europe."[2] The treaty aimed at promoting "economic and social progress [...], in particular through the creation of an area without internal frontiers, through the strengthening of economic and social cohesion and through the establishment of economic and monetary union, ultimately including a single currency [...]." In addition, the treaty mentioned as objective the assertion of Union's "identity on the international scene, in particular through the implementation of a common foreign and security policy [...]."[3] While democratic consolidation and emerging market economies in Eastern Europe already had a great political and economic effect on Germany in the 1990s, the foreseeable enlarge-

---

1 Bulmer, S. & Paterson, W. E. 2013. Germany as the EU's reluctant hegemon? Of economic strength and political constraints. *Journal of European Public Policy* 20(10), p. 1387.

2 Article A. Treaty on European Union 1992. *Official Journal of the European Communities* C 191, p. 4.

3 Article B. Treaty on European Union 1992. *Official Journal of the European Communities* C 191, p. 4.

ment of the European Union in the 2000s up to 28 member states along with the emergence of differentiated integration shaped a new environment in which Germany was embedded.

Germany as the Union's largest country with close political and economic ties to Eastern Europe was expected to experience a huge change not only in its strategic and political position within the Union, but also in its economic development, industrial ties, investment strategies and labour market. The most recent rounds of enlargement considerably changed the face of European and German politics, respectively, and had an impact on economic development, too. Therefore this article will be split into two parts. The first part will describe and analyze the political effects on Germany as a result of the first two rounds of Eastern European enlargement in 2004 and 2007, disregarding the third one in 2013, incorporating Croatia. One year after Croatia's accession we do not have sufficient data reflecting the effects it might has exerted on Germany. The second part outlines the enlargement effects on German economy and labour market as well as on immigration from Eastern Europe to Germany, which has been the main development obstacle since 2004.

Political effects

The political effects of Eastern European enlargement were most visible in Germany's changed voice and political weight in European and international politics. Germany, which was classified as a semi-sovereign state until reunification,[4] faced many serious confinements in the deployment of political power in Europe and the World, respectively. Thus, constraints on German power in the Cold War era were double: the country was divided into two states and the Western part integrated in a community, "designed to address the potential problems emerging from the re-creation of German industrial power"[5] in the 1950s. Often portrayed as "economic gi-

---

4 Katzenstein, P. (ed.) 1987. *Policy and Politics in Germany: the Growth of a Semis-overeign State.* Philadelphia: Temple University Press; Paterson W. E. 2005. European policy making: between associated sovereignty and semi-sovereignty. In Green S. & Paterson W. E. (eds). *Governance in contemporary Germany.* Cambridge: Cambridge University Press, pp. 261-282.
5 Bulmer, S. & Paterson, W. E. 2013 op. cit., p. 1387.

ant but political dwarf"[6] or a "kind of 'semi-Gulliver'"[7] in the 1970s and 1980s, Germany was always reluctant to fully translate its size and economic potential into political power. Even more, the "Germans have eliminated the concept of 'power' from their political vocabulary", and that indicated "a deeper transformation on both the style and substance of German and European politics."[8] Instead of seeking a strong political leadership, Germany has traditionally preferred to rely on side payments to achieve political goals.[9]

The fall of communism and the German reunification removed many formal constraints, but budgetary restrictions following reunification prohibited further side payments, particularly because of the considerable number of states being potential receivers, the growing demands from poorer states, and Germany's own burden as a consequence of the reunification. All this required a new strategy and a new form of German political behaviour, adequate to a fully sovereign state, but committed to European integration – a policy pursued by Chancellor Helmut Kohl. "Furthermore, the acceleration of the European integration process, illustrated by the Treaty of the European Union, signed in Maastricht in 1991 [the treaty was drafted in December 1991 and signed on 7 February 1992], was, among other things, also a self-conscious French attempt to harness the enhanced power of a united Germany to an international institution that promised to grant France partial control and thus keep the European power balance from shifting too rapidly against France"[10] Therefore, especially France but Italy, too, decided to "bind it [Germany] even more tightly into Europe, through a monetary union"[11] which has been achieved with the signature of the Maastricht Treaty. Nevertheless, the European monetary

---

6 Sperling J. 2001. Neither Hegemony nor Dominance: Reconsidering German Power in Post Cold-War Europe. *British Journal of Political Science* 31(2), pp. 389-425; Bulmer, S. & Paterson, W. E. 2013 op. cit., p. 1388.

7 Bulmer, S. & Paterson, W. E. 1989. West Germany's Role in Europe: 'Man-Mountain' or 'Semi-Gulliver'. *Journal of Common Market Studies* 28(2), 95-117.

8 Katzenstein, P. J. 1997. United Germany in an Integrating Europe. *Tamed Power: Germany in Europe*. Ed. Peter J. Katzenstein. Ithaca: Cornell University Press, p. 2.

9 Paterson, W. E. 2011. The Reluctant Hegemon? Germany Moves Centre Stage in the European Union. *Journal of Common Market Studies* 49, p. 60.

10 Katzenstein, P. J. 1997, op. cit., p. 8-9.

11 Ash, T. G. 2013. The New German Question. The New York Review of Books, August 15.

union as a "European project to constrain Germany"[12] was accepted by German politicians, because "the Germans have so internalized positive interdependence and the negative risks of solo operations that they themselves are seeking not only monetary union but also a political union that would go far beyond any pooling of sovereignty the French or British are prepared to accept."[13]

Insofar, "German unification was a decisive determinant for the simultaneous move towards a deepening and widening of the European integration process."[14] The first Europe-Agreements binding Eastern European countries closer to the European Union were signed one year after the German reunification and parallel to the drafting of the Maastricht Treaty. There was German resistance against the association agreements, mainly due to economic fears but also because of France's opposition which Germany didn't want to oppose openly. However, German Chancellor Kohl had emphasized in March 1991: "The European Community isn't all of Europe. The Community must generally be open to other European countries. [...] But this means, that we don't exclude anyone if the conditions for membership are fulfilled."[15] Retrospectively we can say that Europe-Agreements were notably driven by Germany despite some internal opposition and ambivalent actions, and they also served as the first steps of an active Eastern Enlargement policy, because they were developed as a tool to achieve membership in the Union.

Until 1998, when first accession negotiations started, Germany performed much better than France in developing political and economic ties with Eastern countries. The enlargement project exacerbated both fears of French policy makers, that Germany could become a strong regional player in Europe and could weaken the Franco-German decision-making centre in the European Union. Therefore, French politicians opposed the idea of an enlargement and French president "Mitterrand considered himself in a morally awkward situation as long as he resisted the pressure of the Ger-

---

12 Ibid.
13 Pond, E. 1992. Germany in the New Europe. Foreign Affairs 71(2), p. 116.
14 Katzenstein, P. J. 1996. Regionalism in Comparative Perspective. *Cooperation and Conflict* 31, p. 123-159.
15 Kohl, H. 1991. Solidarität und Bereitschaft zur Verantwortung – Die Rolle Deutschlands in Europa. Vortrag anlässlich der Eröffnung der zweiten Tagung des „Forum für Deutschland" in Berlin. *Bulletin des Presse- und Informationsamts der Bundesregierung* Nr. 33 (22. March 1991).

man and the Central and Eastern European governments to consent to enlargement."[16] Germany had slowly embraced the Eastern enlargement into its foreign policy rationale, for which reason the political and economic impact of the enlargement on Germany started to be effective even before the enlargement itself took place. German foreign policy turned into European policy (*Europapolitik*) and therefore the enlargement's political effects were mainly noticeable in the European sphere. Here the traditional Franco-German integration leadership was complemented by an enlargement strategy driven by Germany, which changed "the previous delicate balance of power in the French-German core of the European integration and it would be more correctly to talk now about the German-French core of the EU."[17] This shift was also confirmed in the economic crisis in 2009 and the time period thereafter.

Despite Germany's increasing political importance the Treaty of Nice,[18] which came into force in 2003, did neither fully reflect Germany's new positioning nor its political interests. The Treaty, necessary for the institutional reform and the Union's functioning after the enlargement, "changed the principle of decision-making in the Council of Ministers from consensus to outvoting dissenting minorities."[19] At the same moment the Treaty established a weighted triple majority system with a parity of votes in the European Council between Germany, France, UK and Italy, assigning 29 votes to each of these countries.[20] This share of vote was implemented despite the fact that Germany has about 82,5 Million inhabitants and Italy – the smallest of the Big Four – only 57,7 Million. Furthermore the vote spread between large and small countries was expanded, but shifted voting portion in favour of medium sized and small countries, especially Spain and later Poland each of both receiving 27 weighted votes.

---

16 Schimmelfennig, F. 2001. The Community Trap: Liberal Norms, Rhetorical Action, and the Eastern Enlargement of the European Union. International Organization 55(1), p. 74.

17 Więcławski, J. 2011. Poland East-Central Europe and the European Union's Policy towards Russia. *International Journal of Humanities and Social Science* 1(4), p. 25.

18 Treaty of Nice amending the Treaty on European Union, the Treaties establishing the European Communities and certain related acts 2001. *Official Journal of the European Communities* C80, pp.1-87.

19 Taylor, P. G. 2008. The End of European Integration: Anti-Europeanism Examined. London: Routledge, p. 70.

20 Treaty of Nice 2001, op. cit., p. 50.

The number of these weighted votes must firstly equal or exceed the threshold of 169 out of 237 (=71,3 per cent), must cover secondly a simple majority of the member countries, and must thirdly represent a superma-jority of 62 per cent of the population. Last stipulation was introduced considering Germany's large population and for the sake of compensating the imbalance in the voting weight system. The effect of the population factor was expected "to boost the voting power of Germany and reduce the voting power of all other members to varying extend [...]. But in all cases – including those of Germany and the six greatest losers – the effect [was] rather small."[21] If we consider distribution of power within the Council by calculating power indices, Germany's large population made no real difference.

Table 1: Voting weight, population and Banzhaf power index[22] before and after the Treaty of Nice

	Votes	share of population in %		√(Pop.) a.e.	Banzhaf power index %					
					be-fore	without population's share		with population's share		
		b.e.	a.e.	in %	Nice	b.e.	a.e.	b.e.	a.e.	
Germany	29	21,71	16,96	9,54	11,16	11,94	7,71450334	12,02	7,71453637	
France	29	15,99	12,49	8,09	11,16	11,94	7,71450334	11,98	7,71452797	
UK	29	15,51	12,12	8,10	11,16	11,94	7,71450334	11,98	7,71452797	
Italy	29	15,25	11,91	7,99	11,16	11,94	7,71450334	11,94	7,71452797	
Spain	27	10,43	8,15	6,61	9,24	11,17	7,37316279	11,17	7,3731697	
Nether-lands	13	4,18	3,27	4,18	5,87	5,87	3,98997981	5,85	3,98997777	
Belgium	12	2,7	2,11	3,37	5,87	5,21	3,70916009	5,19	3,70915731	
Greece	12	2,78	2,17	3,42	5,87	5,21	3,70916009	5,19	3,70915731	
Portugal	12	2,86	2,23	3,33	5,87	5,21	3,70916009	5,19	3,70915731	
Austria	10	2,14	1,68	2,99	4,79	4,52	3,11260835	4,5	3,11260398	
Sweden	10	2,59	2,03	3,13	4,79	4,52	3,11260835	4,5	3,11260398	

---

21 Felsenthal, D. S. & Machover, M. 2001. The Treaty of Nice and qualified majority voting. Social Choice and Welfare 18, p. 439.
22 Kirsch, W. 2001. Mathematik und politische Macht. Der EU-Gipfel von Nizza und die Machtstrukturen im Europäischen Rat. *DMV-Mitteilungen* 1, p. 19-20; Leech, D. 2002. Designing the voting system for the Council of the European Union. Public Choice 113, p. 453; Felsenthal, D. S. & Machover, M. 2001. op. cit., p. 448-453. Different index values may have resulted from different statistical data, like population figures.

	Votes	share of population in %		√(Pop.) a.e.	Banzhaf power index %				
					before Nice	without population's share		with population's share	
		b.e.	a.e.	in %	Nice	b.e.	a.e.	b.e.	a.e.
Denmark	7	1,4	1,10	2,43	3,59	2,97	2,19842515	2,96	2,19841836
Finland	7	1,35	1,05	2,39	3,59	2,97	2,19842515	2,96	2,19841836
Ireland	7	0,98	0,77	2,04	3,59	2,97	2,19842515	2,96	2,19841836
Luxemburg	4	0,11	0,09	0,69	2,26	1,64	1,26028071	1,61	1,26027144
Poland	27		7,98	6,55			7,37316279		7,37316970
Romania	14		4,69	4,99			4,27708610		4,27708482
Czech Rep.	12		2,13	3,38			3,70916009		3,70915731
Hungary	12		2,07	3,35			3,70916009		3,70915731
Bulgaria	10		1,65	3,02			3,11260835		3,11260398
Slovakia	7		1,14	2,45			2,19842515		2,19841836
Lithuania	7		0,77	2,03			2,19842515		2,19841836
Cyprus	4		0,15	0,91			1,26028071		1,26027144
Estonia	4		0,03	1,27			1,26028071		1,26027144
Latvia	4		0,52	1,64			1,26028071		1,26027144
Slovenia	4		0,41	1,48			1,26028071		1,26027144
Malta	3		0,08	0,65			0,95144037		0,95143028
Total	345	100*	100*	100*	100*	100*	100	100	100

b.e. = before enlargement, a.e. = after enlargement. $\sqrt{Pop.}$ = indexes by calculating the square-root of total population in a country in order to find proper voting weights.

* rounded to 100.

The table above shows that Germany's voting power was marginally increased by the Treaty of Nice at 0.78 per cent. Germany's relative voting power remained the same as the ones of France, the UK and Italy without taking population factor into account, but was raised at the expense of the smaller countries. The biggest winner was Spain, which increased its voting power from 9,24 to 11,17 per cent. But the Banzhaf power index in Table 1 also shows that population factor's impact on German voting power was marginal even before enlargement, counting at 0.04 per cent. But after enlargement it had neither practical nor theoretical significance, because difference between Germany and France diminished to $8,4^{-8}$ per cent. This marginally higher index value means in reality that the population factor would statistically become effective every 12,5 Million votings.[23] Insofar, the enlargement visibly reduced both, Germany's voting power as well as its structural political weight and did "not give Germany measurably more voting power than to the UK, France and Italy – contrary to the apparent intention of the authors of the Treaty of Nice."[24] This happened due to the fact that after the enlargement the majority threshold increased to 255 out of 345 votes, that is 73,9 per cent of votes in the Council, which "confirms that all members, most significantly the largest countries, suffer[ed] a loss of influence."[25]

The voting system introduced with the Treaty of Nice had several drawbacks, like the "very small decision-making efficiency", which "is defined as the probability that a proposal will be passed by the Council. The value of this quantity [was] very low (about 2.03 per cent)."[26] German politicians were aware of Germany's diminishing voting power and were able to exert real political influence via diplomatic means[27] through well-established political contacts to new member states behind the scene. Controversial discussions on voting weights and voting power started immediately after and led to a reconfiguration, which took effect in the Treaty of Lisbon, signed on 13 December 2007. Especially Germany gained more voting power at the expense of medium sized states without changing the established voting weights in the Council.[28]

The rules for decision-making were considerably improved by the Treaty of Lisbon, and the above mentioned triple majority rule was replaced by a simplified double majority system. The Treaty prescribes that as from 1 November 2014 "a qualified majority shall be defined as at least 55 per cent of the members of the Council representing the participating Member States, comprising at least 65 per cent of the population of these States. A blocking minority must include at least four Council members,

---

23 Kirsch, W. 2001. op. cit., p. 20.
24 Felsenthal, D. S. & Machover, M. 2001. op. cit., p. 462.
25 Leech, D. 2002. op. cit., p. 454.
26 Kirsch,W. & Langner J. 2011. Invariably Suboptimal: An Attempt to Improve the Voting Rules of the Treaties of Nice and Lisbon. *Journal of Common Market Studies* 49(6), p. 1321.
27 Więcławski, J. 2010. The Eastern Enlargement of the European Union: Fears, Challenges, and Reality. Globality Studies Journal 15, p. 4.
28 Treaty of Lisbon amending the Treaty on European Union and the Treaty establishing the European Community, signed at Lisbon, 13 December 2007. *Official Journal of the European Union* 50(C306), pp. 163-163.

failing which the qualified majority shall be deemed attained."[29] In addition, another threshold of 72 per cent for special decisions as well as a transitional period from 1 November 2014 to 31 March 2017[30] was implemented, but these aspects will not be discussed in this context. The overall decreased threshold for the majority-building process in terms of Council members, and the upgraded weighing of the population criterion significantly changed Germany's voting power and thus its political influence in the Council. The different outcomes of the different rules also explain why Poland lobbied for the so-called Penrose Square-Root Rule. Changes in voting power by the Treaty of Lisbon and the Square-Root method are illustrated in Figure 1. Calculations on voting power proof Germany's increasing political voice and influence after enlargement and the reform of the Treaty of Nice. From 2015 onwards and especially after 2017, when the transitional period will expire, Germany will obviously become the biggest voting power winner within the European Union. Of course, this gain in political voice and influence is a relative one, because an enlarging European Union leads to a decreasing absolute voting share for each country. But the former parity of voting power between the Big Four was changed in favour of the population share and thus institutionally granting Germany more voting power and more political influence on the European stage than before. Table 2 illustrates the changes in voting power introduced by the Treaty of Lisbon. Nevertheless, despite all these changes Germany's overall representation on European stage does neither totally reflect the country's political and economic importance nor do they fairly consider its large population on all European stages.

---

29 Article 9c, Treaty of Lisbon, op. cit. 18.
30 Treaty of Lisbon, op. cit. 104 and 159-161.

Table 2: Banzhaf-power index according to provisions in the Treaty of Nice and Treaty of Lisbon, respectively, and according to the Penrose Square-Root Rule[31]

Member state	Total popu-lation	√(Pop.) absolute	√(Pop.) in %	Banzhaf-power in-dex acc. to Treaty of Lisbon in %	Banzhaf-power in-dex acc. to Treaty of Nice in %
Germany	82.221.808	9.067,6242	9,4108	11,5362	7,7828
France	63.753.140	7.984,5563	8,2867	9,0667	7,7828
UK	61.185.981	7.822,1468	8,1181	8,7322	7,7827
Italy	59.618.114	7.721,2767	8,0135	8,5360	7,7827
Spain	45.283.259	6.729,2837	6,9839	6,6893	7,4199
Poland	38.115.641	6.173,7866	6,4074	5,6050	7,4198
Romania	21.528.627	4.639,8951	4,8155	4,1306	4,2591
Netherlands	16.404.282	4.050,2200	4,2035	3,4952	3,9740
Greece	11.214.992	3.348,8792	3,4756	2,8747	3,6843
Belgium	10.666.866	3.266,0168	3,3896	2,8092	3,6843
Portugal	10.617.575	3.258,4621	3,3818	2,8033	3,6843
Czech Republic	10.381.130	3.221,9761	3,3439	2,7750	3,6843
Hungary	10.045.000	3.169,3848	3,2893	2,7349	3,6843
Sweden	9.182.927	3.030,3345	3,1450	2,6321	3,0924
Austria	8.331.930	2.886,5083	2,9957	2,5302	3,0924
Bulgaria	7.640.238	2.764,098	2,8687	2,4478	3,0924
Denmark	5.475.791	2.340,0408	2,4286	2,1891	2,1809
Slovak Republic	5.400.998	2.324,0047	2,4119	2,1803	2,1809
Finland	5.300.484	2.302,278	2,3894	2,1681	2,1809
Ireland	4.419.859	2.102,3461	2,1819	2,0625	2,1809
Lithuania	3.366.357	1.834,7635	1,9042	1,9362	2,1809
Latvia	2.270.894	1.506,9486	1,5640	1,8044	1,2502
Slovenia	2.025.866	1.423,3292	1,4772	1,7747	1,2502
Estonia	1.340.935	1.157,9875	1,2018	1,6920	1,2502
Cyprus	794.580	891,3922	0,9251	1,6260	1,2502
Luxembourg	483.799	695,5566	0,7219	1,5886	1,2502
Malta	410.584	640,7683	0,6650	1,5796	0,9422
Total	497.481.657	96.353,8647	100,00	100,00	100,00

Banzhaf-power index in Table 2 differs from that in Table 1 due to other statistical data, especially the shares of population.

---

31 Kirsch, W. & Langner, J. 2011. op. cit. pp. 1327 and 1329.

Figure 1: Changes in Voting Power and Penrose Square-Root Rule

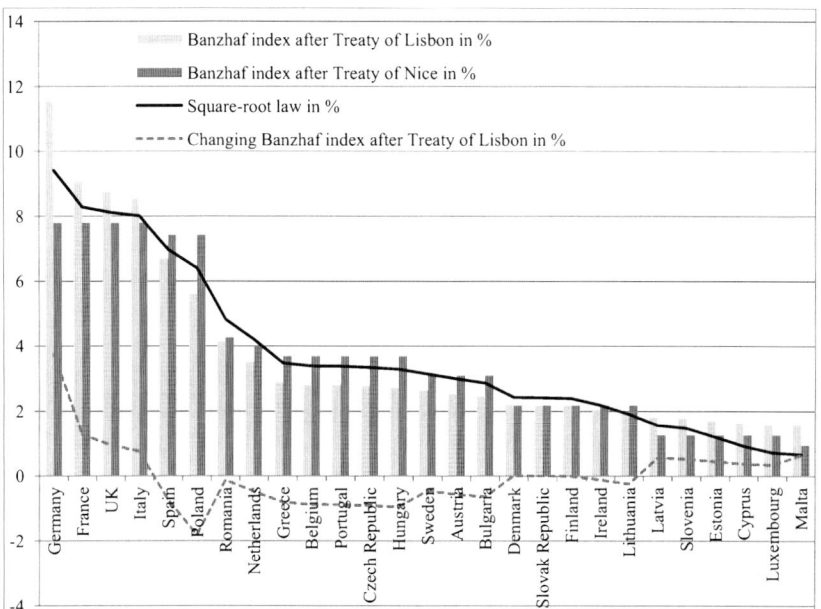

But, on the European scene the "idea of 'solo' German leadership was re-garded as unacceptable to the other member states, and France was the es-sential partner, if Germany was to fulfil its 'European vocation'. The struggle over the ratification of the Lisbon Treaty placed large question marks against the last two reasons. In the efforts to salvage the Treaty oth-er Member States had looked to German leadership. After ratification had been achieved the appetite for more integration and joint action appeared sated. It was the onset of the Eurozone crisis that really exposed the limi-tations of the Franco-German relationship."[32] German-French dynamics dramatically slowed down after the downturn of the French economy and controversial opinions between conservative German and socialist French government, with the latter stepping off the European stage in order to get its affairs back in order. Spain lost its financial credibility and even Italy has fallen far behind, suffering from structural deficiencies and an enor-mous public debt. The UK, which suffered from the crisis, too, but was

---

32 Bulmer & Paterson 2013. op. cit., p. 1394.

Ralf Thomas Göllner

somewhat sheltered by the British Pound, refused to play an active political role and to assist Germany on the European stage, fearing repercussions on British economy. Insofar Germany lost many traditional political partners and this explains why Germany's relations to new Member Countries, especially Poland, turned out to be crucial for securing Germany's influence on European politics. Contrary to Southern European Member States, most new Member Countries were in line with German austerity policy, emphasizing budgetary discipline and cost-saving reforms. According to the results of a survey conducted in Poland in 2012, the "Poles in their majority support the position of the German government that the countries in financial troubles should implement austerity measures (62 per cent)."[33]

This fight against the financial crisis and an affinity across the 150-million-strong Central Europe was seen as a good example for the EU as a whole, and as a potential new motor for the entire Union. Despite the difficult history and recent dissonances especially regarding Germany's close relations to Russia, Poland gained growing importance in German political concepts especially after 2007, when Poland was breaking with its reputation as a blocking state. This appears to be understandable, because Poland as a non-Euro-country has also emerged well from the financial crisis and shares many of Germany's policy priorities. Some analysts even talked about a new German-Polish congenial relationship[34], relocating Europe's core area to the East. For Poland, the "UK had become a liability, undermining the efforts of non-Eurozone members to affect decisions. France had gained a formal basis for excluding Poland. And Germany was emerging as the guarantor of its inclusion and thus for Poland's catch-up."[35] But Polish strategic concerns sometimes trump its economic interests, as the current Ukraine-crisis shows, and Germany is today not able to efficiently influence European politics without its traditional partner France. Insofar, the emergence of a Polish-German tandem on the European stage is "a matter of engagement, endurance and hard work. These days at least, Ger-

---

33 Łada, A. 2012. The Poles on Polish-German Relations and Germany's Role in Europe. Main conclusions. p. 2.

34 Wood, St. 2002a. Apprehensive Partners: Germany, Poland and EU Enlargement. *German* Politics 11(1), pp. 97-124.

35 Parkes, R. 2013. How Poland Came to Be a Major EU Power. *Strategic Europe.* online available: http://carnegieeurope.eu/strategiceurope/?fa=51958 (last visit: 22 July 2014).

many and Poland seem more committed to delivering on concepts, ideas and political commitment to Europe than anybody else. Germany meanwhile needs a strong partner in Europe. [...] German institutional ideas for a 'more' and a better Europe were always generally well accepted when they came accompanied and thereby, sublimated; usually by France. But they cannot arrive alone and Poland today has already largely replaced France as a German tandem partner, when it comes to institutional ideas for Europe."[36]

This is the main caveat in the political effect of enlargement: On the one hand, Germany gained a substantial increase in voice and political influence on the European stage as well as more political comrades in Eastern Europe. "In short, enlargement has sharpened the appreciation of Germany's distinctive interests."[37] On the other hand, socio-political and economic demands due to enlargement and – to a greater extend – the economic crisis since 2009 created the paradox situation that Europe demanded German leadership while at the same moment many believed the country to be "too powerful" for Europe.[38]

Economic effects

Measuring political power and political effects in a changing environment is not an easy undertaking, especially with only few data. It is in contrast much more promising to analyze economic effects of Eastern European enlargement, because we have comprehensive data for example on trade, foreign direct investments in new Member Countries or migration to Germany, which can be classified as economic, political and social parameters in an enlargement and crisis-scenario. Many of the economic effects could be observed years before the Eastern European enlargement actually occurred. The Europe Agreements opened Eastern and Western European markets by reducing trade barriers and tariffs. This had remarkable effects

---

36 Gebert, K. & Guérot, U. 2012. Why Poland is the new France for Germany. *open-Democracy.* online available: https://www.opendemocracy.net/ulrike-guerot-kon-stanty-gebert/why-poland-is-new-france-for-germany (last visit: 22 July 2014).

37 Paterson, W. E. 2011. op. cit., p. 61.

38 Jeffries, St. 2013. Is Germany too powerful for Europe? The Guardian 31 March. online available: http://www.theguardian.com/world/2013/mar/31/is-germany-too-powerful-for-europe (last visit: 22 July 2014).

on trade and direct investments in Eastern European countries mainly "because of the considerable sectoral variation among Germany's industries and those of the CEECs [Central Eastern European Countries]."[39]

Nevertheless, the EU enlargement was not unanimously favoured by the German public, due to the fear of rising net contributions to Union's budget, growing immigration and increasing unemployment.[40]. But the effects of complete single-market access after accession, "reflected in reductions of real trade costs, were even greater than those of the tariff cuts agreed in the Europe Agreements, since they were symmetrical for imports and exports",[41] and meant an improvement for Germany in terms of trade. Thus, while German trade has already improved over the years, the Eastern European enlargement introduced an additional stimulus. How spectacular the German export to new Member Countries developed over the years can be shown best when comparing with France and the UK, two other big countries in the Union. The following Figure 2 shows German, French and British exports in Eastern European New Member States from 1993 to 2013.

It is obvious that Germany was able to establish sooner and closer economic relationships to Eastern European countries than France and the UK. This can partly be explained with Germany's favourable geographic location, but – and this is more important – with the structural and cultural benefits, its early entry into the Eastern European markets, and its development of long lasting ties not only by large enterprises but also by small and medium sized companies. Thus, even the economic crisis after 2009 could not exert a long lasting negative effect on the German trade with new Member Countries.

But Germany is not only the largest export country within the European Union, it is the most important importer of Eastern European goods, too.

---

39 Ochmann, R. R. 2005. The First EU Eastern Enlargement. Impacts on the German Economy and the Public Perceptions. *Institute for World Economics, Hungarian Academy of Science, Working Papers* 158, p. 11.

40 As an example for the discussions Wood, St. 2002b. Germany and the Eastern Enlargement of the EU: Political Elites, Public Opinion and Democratic Processes. *Journal of European Integration* (24)1, pp. 23-38. Wood, St. 2003. Is Eastern Enlargement of the European Union a Beneficial Investment for Germany? Political Science Quarterly 118(2), pp. 281-306. Schuck, A. R. T. & de Vreese, C. H. 2006. Between Risk and Opportunity: News Framing and its Effects on Public Support for EU Enlargement. *European Journal of Communication* 21(5), pp. 5-32.

41 Ochmann, R. R. 2005. op. cit. p. 12.

The following Figure 3 shows the terms of trade and illustrates that German imports from Eastern Europe grew nearly at the same rate as the corresponding exports.

Figure 2: French, German and British total Exports of Goods in Eastern European New Member States (1993-2013)

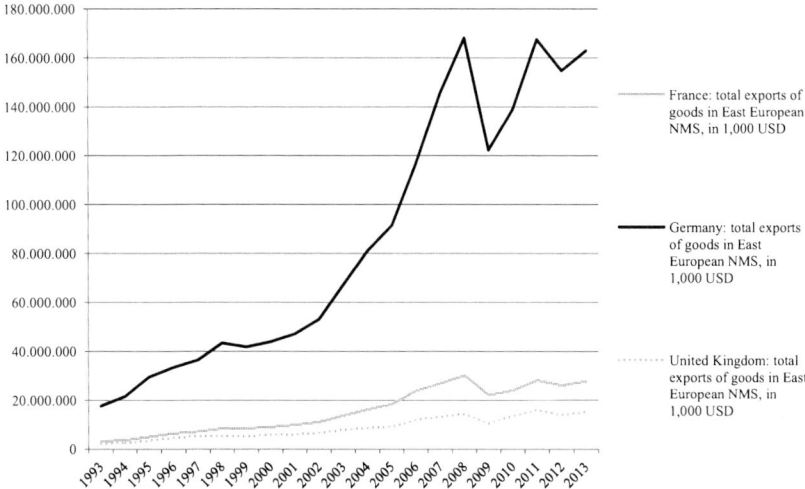

(Data by OECD, http://stats.oecd.org/, last accessed: 18 June 2014)

Figure 3: German Terms of Trade and Eastern European New Member States (1995-2013)

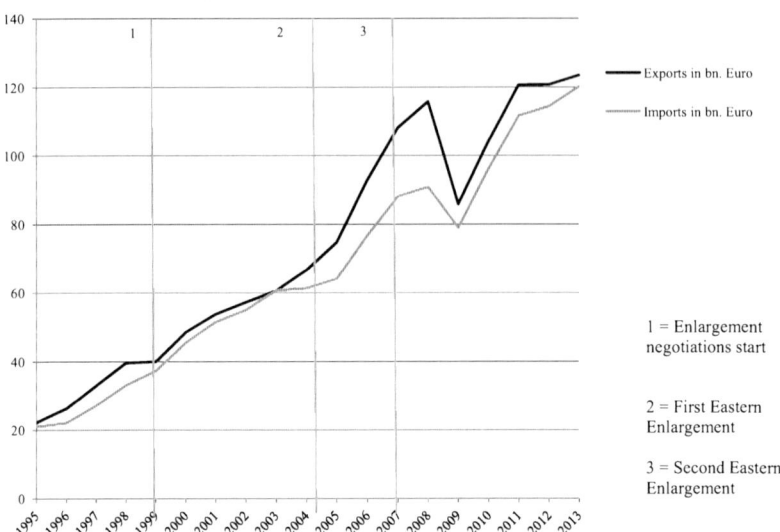

(Data by OECD, http://stats.oecd.org/, last accessed: 18 June 2014)

This observation can be explained partly with economic reforms the Eastern European New Member Countries had carried out for more than one decade, and partly with the increasing interdependence of Eastern European economies, which "have become deeply embedded into Western European markets and production structures."[42] Almost all Eastern European New Member Countries are important suppliers of semi-finished goods especially in the automotive sector and therefore important partners for the German automotive industry. Furthermore, the advantages resulting from national currencies helped reducing the problems stemming from external imbalances. The increasing payments from the EU budget, namely in the framework of the cohesion policy after 2004, also stabilized Eastern European economies and led to an increasing European division of labour. This is an argument for a structural growing together of German and Eastern European economies, mainly driven by previous German investments in those countries prior to their actual accession. Interestingly,

---

42 Medve-Bálint, Gy. 2014. The Role of the EU in Shaping FDI Flows to East Central Europe. *Journal of Common Market Studies* 52(1), p. 48.

the second enlargement in 2007, involving Bulgaria and Romania, had no significant economic effect on Germany.

French and British imports did not perform nearly as good and were not constantly growing as the German ones, despite the fact that the UK has been – unlike France – an early and strong driver of Eastern European enlargement. The similar trade volumes of the UK and France with Eastern European countries and their different stances on EU enlargement suggest that their positions were mainly motivated by political considerations and to a lesser extent by economic ones.[43] Nevertheless, especially Germany but the UK, too, benefited from EU enlargement even if the channels – trade in goods and services, movement of capital and the migration of labour – "by which these gains have been achieved differ. While the gains from enlargement are trade driven in Germany, they result mainly from the opening of the labour market in United Kingdom."[44] France, which neither substantially improved trade with Eastern European countries nor attracted large numbers of qualified work force from Europe's East, benefited least among the Big Four from Eastern European enlargement. The following Figure 4 illustrates German, British and French imports from Eastern European New Member states since 1993 and once again reveals Germany as Eastern Europe's most important economic partner and that "the gains from enlargement are trade driven in Germany."

43 See Schimmelfennig, F. 2001. op. cit.

44 Baas, T. & Brücker, H. 2010. Macroeconomic impact of Eastern enlargement on Germany and UK: evidence from a CGE model. Applied Economics Letters 17(2), p. 127.

Figure 4: Germany, France, the UK: Total imports of goods from Eastern European NMS

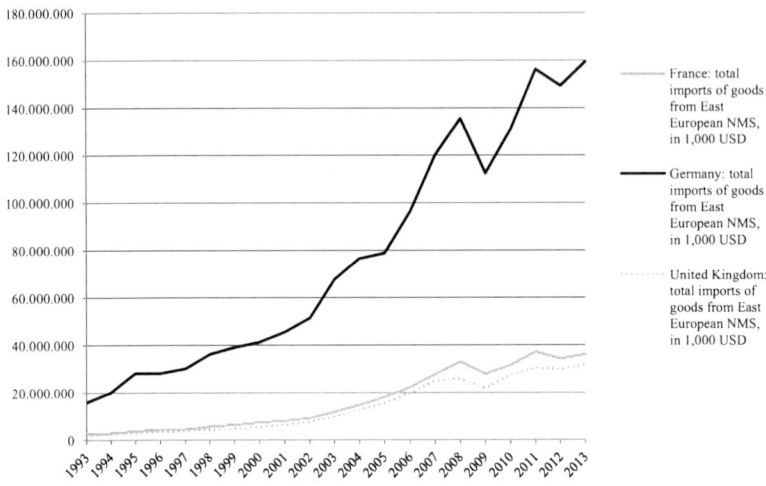

(Data by OECD, http://stats.oecd.org/, last accessed: 18 June 2014)

Figure 5: German Foreign Trade and the Visegrád-countries

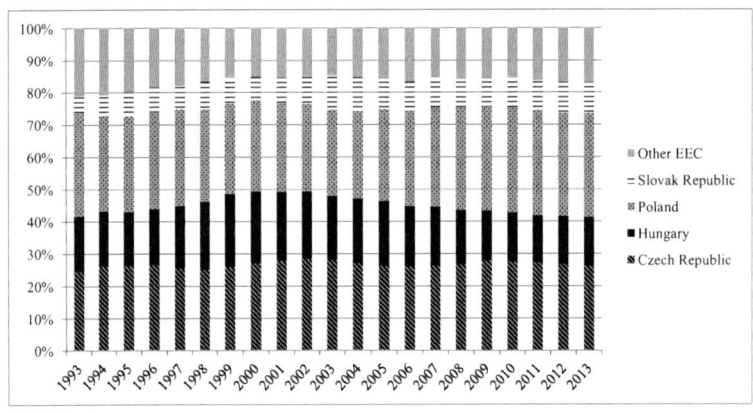

(Data by OECD, http://stats.oecd.org/, last accessed: 18 June 2014)

Obviously, German trade has never been equally allocated to all countries concerned. There seems to be a trade preference aiming at Central Eastern Visegrád-countries. These are in order of trade importance: Poland, the Czech Republic, Hungary and the Slovak Republic, covering more than 80 percent of German trade in the Eastern European region in 2013 (see figure 5).

The continuously rising importance of the new Member States is also visible in Germany's changed foreign trade ranking. While France, the UK, and the United States of America (until 2002) used to be Germany's most important trade partners, the EU enlargement paved the way for the Eastern European New Member States to take on the leading role in German foreign trade. Figure 6 displays the rising importance of the Eastern European countries for German foreign trade from 2004 onwards. The impressive growth rate nicely reflects the positive effects of single market's Eastern European enlargement on Germany. Table 3 illustrates the ranking of Germany's selected trading partners in 2013. The statistics reveals that Germany's total trade with Eastern European New Member States has nearly gained the importance of its trade with the UK und the USA altogether.

Figure 6: Germany and it's volumes of foreign trade in the years 1993-2013

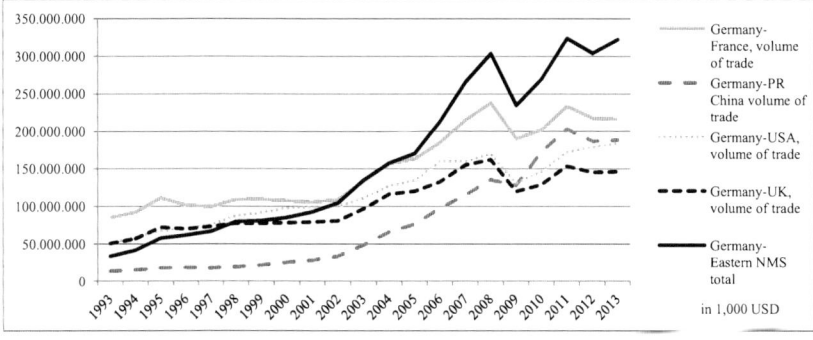

(Data by OECD, http://stats.oecd.org/, last accessed: 18 June 2014)

Table 3: Ranking of selected top trading partners of Germany in 2013, preliminary results[45]

	Exports			Imports			Total Trade	
Rank	Country	Volume in €	Rank	Country	Volume in €	Rank	Country	Volume in €
1	France	100.184.143	1	Netherlands	89.207.743	1	France	164.270.870
2	USA	88.375.078	2	PR of China	73.645.318	2	Netherlands	160.187.716
3	United Kingdom	75.649.570	3	France	64.068.047	3	PR of China	140.638.447
4	Netherlands	70.950.757	4	USA	48.449.725	4	USA	136.830.080
5	PR of China	67.025.440	6	United Kingdom	42.492.548	5	United Kingdom	118.178.054
9	Poland	42.404.308	11	Poland	35.894.767	10	Poland	78.317.899
13	Czech Republic	31.053.546	12	Czech Republic	33.038.634	12	Czech Republic	64.099.833
16	Hungary	17.470.001	15	Hungary	19.492.637	14	Hungary	36.961.487
21	Slovakia	10.654.170	18	Slovakia	12.262.536	20	Slovakia	22.914.789
23	Romania	9.623.963	21	Romania	9.189.367	23	Romania	18.801.022
41	Slovenia	4.092.639	34	Slovenia	4.615.624	37	Slovenia	8.722.010
47	Bulgaria	2.648.630	43	Bulgaria	2.718.372	48	Bulgaria	5.364.512
48	Lithuania	2.469.611	49	Lithuania	1.740.541	52	Lithuania	4.210.152
57	Estonia	1.682.294	69	Latvia	637.580	64	Estonia	2.182.043
61	Latvia	1.428.389	73	Estonia	499.749	66	Latvia	2.065.969
	Eastern NMS total	123.527.551		Eastern NMS total	120.089.807		Eastern NMS total	243.639.716

But not only Germany's trade with Eastern European New Member Countries improved after accession. "Foreign direct investment (FDI) has been one of the main drivers of economic restructuring in east central [sic!] Europe (ECE) and significantly contributed to the region's integration into the European and global markets."[46] In the 1990s capital inflow to the transforming countries in Eastern Europe remained relatively low due to legal and economic uncertainty. But after the introduction of far-reaching reforms, the incipient implementation of the European *acquis communautaire*, and the accession and almost complete compliance with European norms and standards especially German FDI increased notably due to higher legal certainty (see Figure 7). "Yet, only ten years after joining the

---

45 Federal Statistical Office 2014. Foreign Trade. Ranking of Germany's trading partners in foreign trade. Wiesbaden: Statistisches Bundesamt, August 20, 2014.
46 Medve-Bálint, Gy. 2014. op. cit., p. 35.

European Union (EU), the new east [sic!] European members show higher levels of economic internationalization than the old ones."[47]

Figure 7: Germany's foreign direct investment outward flow, in million US-$

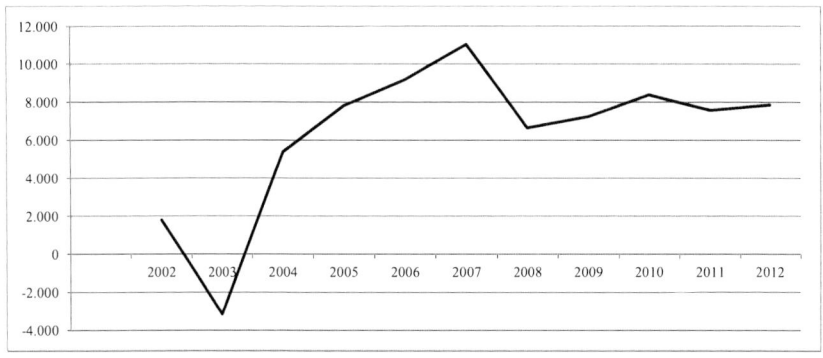

(OECD International Direct Investment Statistics 2013, OECD Publishing)

If we analyse the FDI positions Germany holds in new Member States, the constantly rising importance of Eastern European countries' becomes obvious, even if Eastern European New Member Countries attracted only about 12 per cent of Germany's worldwide FDI outflows in 2012.[48] Starting with accession, German direct investments in Eastern European Countries surpassed those of France. There are multiple reasons which we cannot elaborate on, as it would exceed the objective of this study. But it is important to mention that these rising direct investments have brought Eastern European countries closer to Germany, as they have played an important role in economic internationalization. Furthermore, reinvested earnings gained more significance after accession, suggesting that "foreign businesses have generally turned profitable and the multinational companies in the region are likely to plan long-term operations."[49] However, there is no uniform FDI sector allocation in Eastern Europe. "In the Visegrád 4 (and Slovenia), FDI targeted manufacturing, including in [sic!] automotive, electronic and chemical industries. In contrast, FDI in Bulgar-

---

47 Medve-Bálint, Gy. 2014. op. cit., p. 35.
48 OECD, http://stats.oecd.org/ (last visit: 4 September 2014).
49 Medve-Bálint, Gy. 2014. op. cit., p. 47.

ia, Romania and the Baltic states was concentrated in non-tradable sectors, such as banking and real estate [...]."[50] This general observation specifically applies to German investments, as illustrated by the paramount important sector of German automotive industry. The major German car producers shifted substantial production capacity to Eastern Europe since the mid 1990s, thus integrating important industrial production in Eastern Europe into their value chain. The following Figure 8 shows Germany's FDI positions at year's end, comparing Eastern European New Member States and France.

Figure 8: Germany's FDI positions at year's end in Eastern European NMS and France, in million US-$

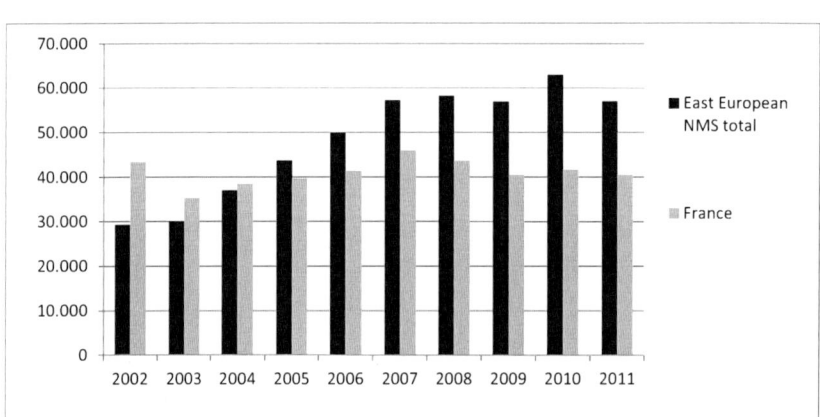

(Data by OECD, http://stats.oecd.org/, last accessed: 18 June 2014)

However, the German FDI outflow especially to Central Eastern European (CEE) countries also had some minor negative effects on Germany. While FDI in financial and real estate services was strategically important and mostly market-oriented, about 40 per cent of German FDI in Eastern European countries were at least partially cost-oriented[51] and thus threatened German labour market by much lower labour costs. Though, "within

---

50 Epstein, R. A. 2014. Overcoming 'Economic Backwardness' in the European Union. *Journal of Common Market Studies* 52(1), p. 25.

51 Dey, C. 2003. Direktinvestitionen in den mittel- und osteuropäischen Beitrittsländern: Rückwirkungen auf den deutschen Arbeitsmarkt? *Wirtschaft im Wandel* 9(4), pp. 103-104.

the sector there has been a clear transition in the nature of inward FDI from the end of the 1990s, which reflects the process of EU integration, as a 'second wave' of investment replaced an earlier wave of labour-intensive activities with more human-capital intensive ones."[52] Insofar, "investment in the NMSs has not involved job cuts in the German sites – although these have later come under strong competitive pressure."[53] In turn, this pushed German production chains' modernization ahead.

Figure 9: Unemployment rate in Germany, 1993-2013

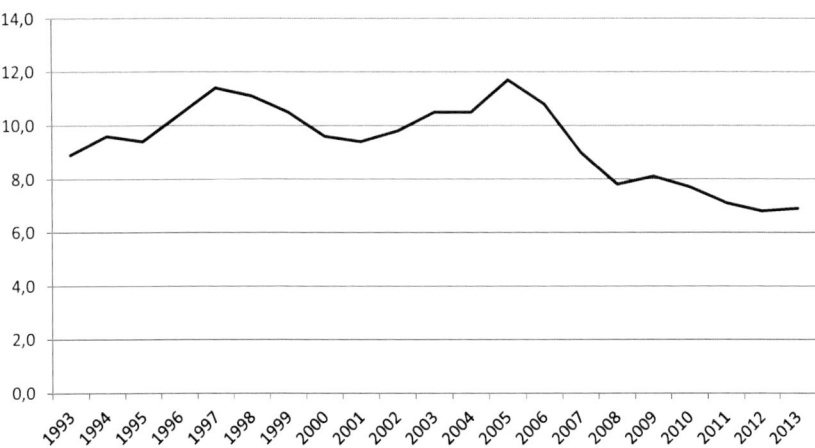

(Data by Bundesagentur für Arbeit, Statistik: Arbeitslosigkeit im Zeitverlauf. Nuremberg, 23. April 2014)

The EU enlargement itself had no special impact on German labour market, as illustrated in Figure 9. Germany's unemployment rate peaked one year after enlargement, but started to decrease shortly thereafter. Although, this was more due to an internal effect resulting from German reform policy when the slowed-down German economy began to recover. In addition, production in Germany and Eastern European New Member States was already interleaved to a large extent in 2004, and the constantly growing demand from Eastern Europe helped reducing unemployment in

---

52 Meardi, G. et al. 2009. The Complexity of Relocation and the Diversity of Trade Union Responses: Efficiency-oriented Foreign Direct Investment in Central Europe. *European Journal of Industrial Relations* 15(1), p. 30.
53 Meardi, G. et al. 2009. op. cit., p. 40.

Germany even after the financial crisis hit European labour markets and economies in 2009. Further, "all but three EU15 countries (the UK, Ireland and Sweden) made use of transitional measures in 2004 restricting – to varying degrees – the right to work for EU8 citizens [the Eastern European new Member Countries without Bulgaria and Romania, which acceded the EU in 2007] in those countries for a period of up to seven years."[54] But only Germany and Austria maximally restricted access for EU8 workers to their domestic labour markets according to the so-called "2+3+2 formula",[55] that is until May 2011 for countries acceded in 2004 and until January 2014 for Romania and Bulgaria, respectively. Whether this foreclosure of German labour market was really successful can be doubted, even if during the economic crisis "EU10 migrants were harder hit in the majority of EU15 countries and acted, at least partially, as labour market buffers."[56] Consequently, many studies on the German labour market conclude that "the potential effects of migration on wages and unemployment are small. [...] It is therefore unlikely that an opening of the labour market will aggravate imbalances in the German labour market substantially."[57]

In consequence, the immigration barriers to German labour market redirected migration flows from Germany and led to higher migration rates especially to the UK and Ireland. While in the year 2000 a total of 434,603 out of 706,295 foreign residents from the EU8 lived in Germany, the ma-

---

54 Galgóczi, B. & Leschke, J. 2014. Post-Enlargement Intra-EU Labour Mobility Under Stress Test. *Intereconomics* 49(3), p. 152.

55 This formula means, that „for the first two years following accession, access to the labor markets of the incumbent member states depends on their national laws and policies. National measures may be extended for a further period of three years and could continue for a further two years, but only if there are serious disruptions in the respective receiving labor market." Kahanec, M. & Zaiceva, A. & Zimmermann, K.F. 2010. Lessons from Migration after EU Enlargement. In: Kahanec, M. & Zimmermann, K. F. (Eds.). *EU Labor Markets After Post-Enlargement Migration*. Heidelberg et al.: Springer, p. 4.

56 Galgóczi, B. & Leschke, J. 2014. op. cit., p. 154.

57 Baas, T. & Brücker, H. 2009. Country Study: Germany. In: Brücker, H. et al. *Labour mobility within the EU in the context of enlargement and the functioning of the transitional arrangements*. Report for the European Commission. Brussels/ Nuremberg, p. 25.

jority can be found in the UK and Ireland after 2006.[58] Figures 10 and 11[59] show the migration directions from EU8 and EU2 (Romania and Bulgaria), respectively, to the most important EU-countries. Migration restrictions in Germany effectively prevented immigration growth from Eastern European New Member States, whereas especially the UK and Ireland "opened up their labour markets from the beginning" and offered "a comparatively favourable labour market situation for the absorption of immigrant labour."[60]

Figure 10: EU8 population (age 15-64) in receiving countries, in thousands

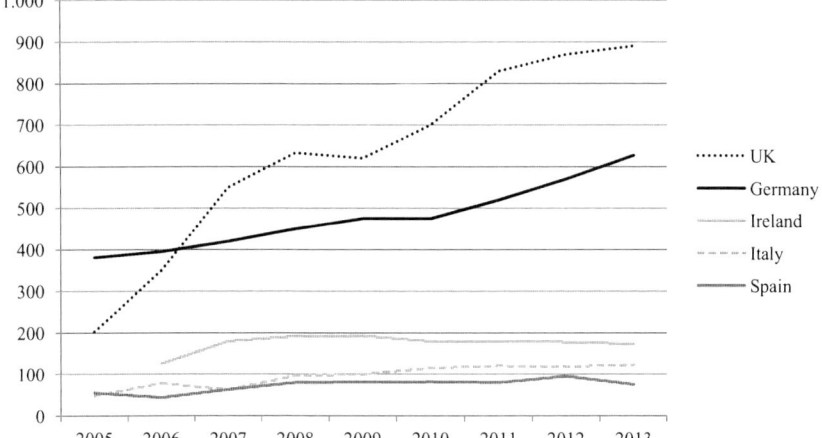

<hr />

58 Brücker, H., et al 2009. Labour mobility within the EU in the context of enlargement and the functioning of the transitional arrangements. Report for the European Commission. Brussels/Nuremberg, p. 24.
59 Galgóczi, B. & Leschke, J. 2014. op. cit., p. 154.
60 Galgóczi, B. & Leschke, J. 2014. op. cit., p. 153.

Figure 11: EU2 population (age 15-64) in receiving countries, in thousands

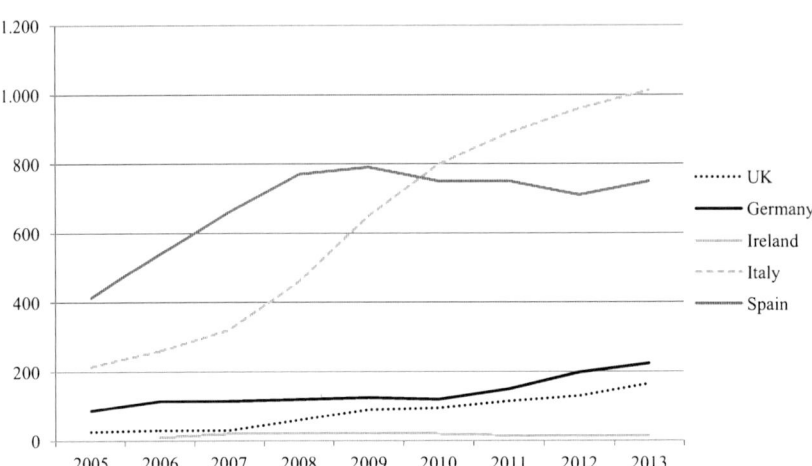

Figure 12 shows the immigration trend to Germany since 1991. The high immigration between 1991 and 2002 is followed by a plateau and moderate decline until 2008, although enlargement had stimulated migration processes. The re-increase of immigration from 2009 onwards reflected Germany's economic performance since the financial crisis of 2009 and the ability to absorb immigration workforce from Eastern European New Members States without harming the domestic labour market and wages. Despite the fact that the labour market restrictions were in force, migration was still possible for example for (sometime bogus) self-employed workers, for exceptional cases like academics or for non-working immigrants. But it was particularly possible for high-skilled workforce, because "in the context of East-West EU labour mobility, specific programmes to attract high-skilled labour and retain graduates from EU10 countries have been important in [...] Germany."[61]

---

61 Galgóczi, B. & Leschke, J. 2014. op. cit., p. 156.

Figure 12: Total immigration to Germany, mid-year term 1991-2013

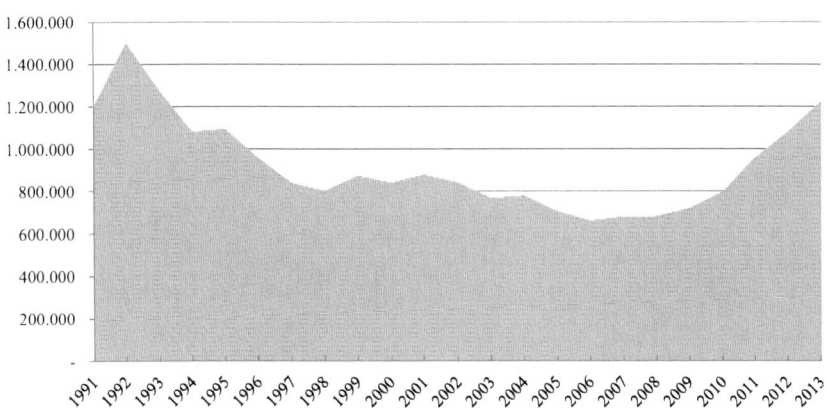

(Statista, http://de.statista.com/statistik/daten/studie/28347/umfrage/zuwanderung-nach-deutschland/, last accessed: 23 July 2015)

Table 4[62] concretizes the stock of immigration from Eastern European New Member States between 2006 und 2013 according to the citizenship of the registered immigrants. The statistics show the overall great number of Polish immigrants in the time period concerned and, more importantly, the multiplying quantity of immigrants from Bulgaria and Romania. While the number of immigrants from the EU8 countries approximately doubled, the number of Bulgarians and Romanians nearly quadrupled. It is interesting to note the large number of women migrating to Germany.

These numbers include all immigrants and not only the job-seeking ones. The substantial increase in the number of immigrants from these countries "raised the issue of the access to social rights by citizens from other EU member states with residence in the given country",[63] especially in Germany and the UK. In these countries, which were affected to a lesser extent by the economic crisis, public fears of the so-called "benefit-tourism"[64] raised up and was sustained by the lasting austerity pressure on municipalities and state budget. Even if "there is no evidence to support

---

62 Statistisches Bundesamt 2014. Bevölkerung und Erwerbstätigkeit. Ausländische Bevölkerung Ergebnisse des Ausländerzentralregisters 2013. Wiesbaden: Statistisches Bundesamt, 24. April 2014, p. 30.
63 Galgóczi, B. & Leschke, J. 2014. op. cit., p. 157.
64 Happold, T. 2004. UK set to act against 'benefit tourism'. The Guardian, Wednesday 4 February.

those fears",[65] with the ongoing crisis in the Eastern European New Member States the unemployment of migrant workers from EU8 slightly raised and a growing number of the unemployed received benefits from the German social security system. Nevertheless, the share of unemployed Eastern Europeans benefiting from the social security system was much lower than the German average as well as and the average of total jobless immigrants. Table 5 illustrates the number of unemployed workers from Eastern European New Member States and the share of total unemployed immigrants.[66] Among those, immigrants from Turkey had the largest share of unemployment, ranging from 26,9 per cent in 2006 to 31,2 per cent in August 2011.[67]

---

65 Galgóczi, B. & Leschke, J. 2014. op. cit., p. 158.
66 Bundesagentur für Arbeit. Arbeitsmarkt in Zahlen. Arbeitssuchende und Arbeitslose nach Staatsangehörigkeit. August 2011, August 2012, August 2013, August 2014. Online: http://statistik.arbeitsagentur.de (last visit: 8 September 2014).
67 Bundesagentur für Arbeit. Arbeitsmarkt in Zahlen. Arbeitssuchende und Arbeitslose nach Staatsangehörigkeit. August 2011, August 2012, August 2013, August 2014, op. cit.

Table 4: Stock of immigrants according to their citizenship and the share of women from Eastern European New Member States between 2006 and 2013

Citizenship	2006 total	2006 Percentage of women	2007 total	2007 Percentage of women	2008 total	2008 Percentage of women	2009 total	2009 Percentage of women	2010 total	2010 Percentage of women	2011 total	2011 Percentage of women	2012 total	2012 Percentage of women	2013 total	2013 Percentage of women
Bulgaria	39.053	57,2	46.818	56,1	53.984	54,6	61.854	53,2	74.869	50,8	93.889	48,2	118.759	46,5	146.828	45,6
Czech Republic	33.316	66,1	34.266	66,3	34.386	66,3	34.337	66,3	35.480	65,5	38.060	64,1	41.865	62,2	46.484	60,5
Estonia	3.970	70,5	4.065	71,3	4.003	71,1	4.108	70,5	4.394	68,8	4.840	67,8	5.224	68,0	5.780	66,1
Hungary	52.347	42,0	56.165	41,1	60.024	40,6	61.417	41,3	68.892	39,7	82.760	38,5	107.398	38,2	135.614	38,3
Latvia	9.775	65,3	9.806	66,6	9.980	66,2	11.650	63,2	14.257	58,8	18.263	55,7	21.790	53,9	25.489	52,7
Lithuania	19.030	70,8	19.833	71,1	20.285	71,1	21.423	70,2	23.522	68,2	27.751	65,1	32.523	62,4	36.316	61,1
Poland	361.696	51,5	384.808	51,2	393.848	51,8	398.513	52,2	419.435	51,5	468.481	49,8	532.375	48,2	609.855	46,9
Romania	73.353	59,3	84.584	56,8	94.326	55,4	104.980	54,5	126.536	51,8	159.222	49,2	205.026	47,1	267.398	45,4
Slovakia	23.835	57,3	24.458	58,3	24.477	58,4	24.930	58,6	26.296	57,8	30.241	55,4	35.372	53,3	41.436	51,7
Slovenia	21.109	50,3	20.971	50,5	20.463	50,9	20.054	51,1	20.034	51,0	20.832	50,1	21.819	48,8	24.094	47,8
Total immigrants from Eastern European NMS	637.484	59,0	685.774	58,9	715.776	58,6	743.266	58,1	813.715	56,4	944.339	54,4	1.122.151	52,9	1.339.294	51,6
Total immigration To Germany	6.751.004	48,5	6.744.879	48,7	6.727.618	48,8	6.694.776	49,0	6.753.621	49,0	6.930.896	48,8	7.213.708	48,6	7.633.628	48,2

Table 5: Benefit recipients from Eastern European New Member States between 2011 and 2014, as of respective year's August

	2011				2012			
	unemployed		jobseeking with relief	receiving benefits	unemployed		jobseeking with relief	receiving benefits
	absolute	percentage	absolute	total	absolute	percentage	absolute	total
Total	2.944.686	7,0	5.119.628	8.064.314	2.905.112	6,8	4.944.237	7.849.349
thereof Germans	2.471.814	6,3	4.284.618	6.756.432	2.423.329	6,2	4.108.943	6.532.272
thereof foreigners	469.119	14,6	827.436	1.296.555	477.721	14,2	828.295	1.306.016
Bulgaria	3.385	0,7	6.967	10.352	4.653	1,0	9.574	14.227
Czech Republic	1.949	0,4	3.768	5.717	2.180	0,5	4.336	6.516
Estonia	259	0,1	495	754	234	0,0	481	715
Hungary	2.009	0,4	3.675	5.684	2.345	0,5	4.507	6.852
Latvia	911	0,2	1.737	2.648	1.098	0,2	2.151	3.249
Lithuania	1.700	0,4	3.195	4.895	1.902	0,4	3.572	5.474
Poland	23.935	5,1	43.353	67.288	26.043	5,5	47.198	73.241
Romania	4.775	1,0	9.318	14.093	5.639	1,2	10.882	16.521
Slovakia	971	0,2	1.840	2.811	1.207	0,3	2.165	3.372
Slovenia	863	0,2	1.447	2.310	827	0,2	1.361	2.188
Eastern European NMS, total	40.757	–	75.795	116.552	46.128	–	86.227	132.355

	2013				2014			
	unemployed		jobseeking with relief	Receiving benefits	unemployed		jobseeking with relief	Receiving benefits
	absolute	percentage	absolute	total	absolute	percentage	absolute	total
Total	2.945.708	6,8	5.019.723	7.965.431	2.901.823	6,7	4.955.533	7.857.356
thereof Germans	2.434.995	6,2	4.130.305	6.565.300	2.366.971	6,0	4.005.035	6.372.006
thereof foreigners	506.529	14,2	882.382	1.388.911	530.569	14,0	943.163	1.473.732
Bulgaria	6.656	1,3	14.300	20.956	11.772	2,2	25.140	36.912
Czech Republic	2.472	0,5	4.807	7.279	2.548	0,5	4.563	7.111
Estonia	300	0,1	603	903	341	0,1	680	1.021
Hungary	3.351	0,7	6.591	9.942	4.341	0,8	8.748	13.089
Latvia	1.388	0,3	2.821	4.209	1.684	0,3	3.325	5.009
Lithuania	2.243	0,4	4.320	6.563	2.537	0,5	5.047	7.584
Poland	30.688	6,1	57.092	87.780	35.115	6,6	66.527	101.642
Romania	7.545	1,5	14.872	22.417	11.465	2,2	24.024	35.489
Slovakia	1.495	0,3	2.774	4.269	1.764	0,3	3.334	5.098
Slovenia	847	0,2	1.500	2.347	950	0,2	1.693	2.643
Eastern European NMS, total	56.985	–	109.680	166.665	72.517	–	143.081	215.598

Therefore, not only immigration numbers changed with accession, the characteristics of immigrants from Eastern European New Member States changed, too. An analysis[68] published by the Institute for the Study of Labor (IZA) in 2013 revealed that until the establishment of the restrictions in 2004 immigrants were on average younger and had a higher educational level than average Germans. As a consequence they had a higher share amongst workers with upper secondary or third-level education. After restrictions had been established, the immigrants characteristics changed. The educational level sank but was still above the German average, while the average earnings and the share of blue-collar workers grew. This high share of medium- and high-skilled persons also explains to some extent the higher employment rate of Eastern European immigrants. The study concludes that many young and well-educated migrants did not go to Germany anymore, so that "the costs of the restrictions exceeded the benefits by far."[69] While immigration restrictions effectively shielded German labour market and wages' structure, they apparently were a detriment for growth of German economy. According to estimations, "the diversion of migration flows increased the GDP, employment growth and total factor income of the native population in the UK whereas Germany could not benefit from an increase in labour."[70] Insofar, the "GDP gains of Germany would have been even larger if it would have opted for a similar immigration policy as United Kingdom, while the gains would have been lower in United Kingdom in this case since it would have attracted a smaller share of migrants."[71] A first turnaround could be observed after the crisis broke out where Germany regained its attractiveness despite immigration restrictions. A second impact followed after abandoning restrictions in 2011 and 2013, respectively, when immigration encountered German economic stability and demand for highly educated, young and flexible workforce.

---

68 Elsner, B. & Zimmermann, K.F. 2013. 10 Years After: EU Enlargement, Closed Borders, and Migration to Germany. *IZA Discussion Paper* 7130. Bonn: IZA.

69 Elsner, B. & Zimmermann, K.F. 2013. op. cit., p. 14.

70 Baas, T. & Brücker, H. 2012. The macroeconomic consequences of migration diversion: Evidence for Germany and the UK. *Structural Change and Economic Dynamics* 23(2), p. 192.

71 Baas, T. & Brücker, H. 2010. op. cit., p. 127.

Conclusions

In a nutshell, the overall effects of the Eastern European enlargement for Germany were exceptionally favourable. Germany's political weight in the European integration process was traditionally counterbalanced by France, Italy and the UK, and it is unlikely that this constellation would have been modified without the Eastern European enlargement. The above described changes in voting power and political voice are closely connected with the enlargement process, scaling down the gap between real political weight and effective voting power. Although the total number of German votes on the European stage declined due to the growing number of member countries, Germany gained more voting weight in comparison to the other big European countries. Insofar, Germany *de facto* benefited in the political sphere through increasing structural and off-the-records influence fired by the reorganisation in the enlargement process. Nevertheless, despite the fact that in the wake of Eastern enlargement changes of voting weights were introduced on the European stage, these reforms of European decision-making processes did not lead to an appropriate reflection of Germany's real political and economic importance in Europe. For Germany, this democratic grievance continuously necessitates the creation of alliances incorporating at least one large country, and Germany gained with Poland a second integration-oriented pillar complementing the traditional French partner on the European scene. The German-Polish partnership could gain more and more importance on the medium term even more in light of increasing instability of French economy and politics, and the rising euro-scepticism in the UK. In addition, most of the Eastern European New Member States have traditionally good relations and strong cultural ties with Germany. These ties and Germany's historical importance for most of the Eastern European countries turned into a structural advantage for their transformation process and the time period thereafter. As a trade-off, Germany also experienced numerous and substantial economic advantages following Eastern European enlargement. These economics gains were primarily trade driven, resulting in an increasing return of capital. But the modernisation of production structures in the face of developing business competitors and production sites in Eastern Europe as well as rising wages in the sequitur of the enlargement process were notable effects, too. The minor impacts on German social security systems and labour markets due to the economic crisis were negligible in light of the benefits. But we must not forget that the fundamentals of German-Eastern

European relationships were laid in the early 1990s, when Germany despite of its struggling with reunification was heavily engaged in supporting the transformation process in post-communist Eastern European countries. Thus, the Eastern European enlargement represents another milestone in the strengthening of the relationship between Germany and Eastern European countries after the breakup of communism.

References

Ash, T. G. 2013. The New German Question. The New York Review of Books, August 15.

Baas, T. & Brücker, H. 2009. Country Study: Germany. In: Brücker, H. et al. *Labour mobility within the EU in the context of enlargement and the functioning of the transitional arrangements*. Report for the European Commission. Brussels/Nuremberg.

Baas, T. & Brücker, H. 2010. Macroeconomic impact of Eastern enlargement on Germany and UK: evidence from a CGE model. *Applied Economics Letters* 17(2), pp. 125-128.

Baas, T. & Brücker, H. 2012. The macroeconomic consequences of migration diversion: Evidence for Germany and the UK. *Structural Change and Economic Dynamics* 23(2), pp. 180-194.

Bulmer, S. & Paterson, W. E. 2013. Germany as the EU's reluctant hegemon? Of economic strength and political constraints. *Journal of European Public Policy* 20(10), pp. 1387-1405.

Bulmer, S. & Paterson, W. E. 1989. West Germany's Role in Europe: 'Man-Mountain' or 'Semi-Gulliver'. *Journal of Common Market Studies* 28(2), pp. 95-117.

Brücker, H. & Baas, T. & Beleva, I. & Bertoli, S. & Boeri, T. & Damelang, A. & Duval, L. & Hauptmann, A. & Fihel, A. & Huber, P. & Iara, A. & Ivlevs, A. & Jahn, E. & Kaczmarczyk, P. & Landesmann, M.E. & Mackiewicz-Lyziak, J. & Makovec, M. & Monti, P. & Nowotny, K. & Okolski, M. & Richter, S. & Upward, R. & Vidovic, H. & Wolf, K. & Wolfeil, N. & Wright, P. & Zaiga, K. & Zylicz, A. 2009. Labour mobility within the EU in the context of enlargement and the functioning of the transitional arrangements. Report for the European Commission. Brussels/Nuremberg.

Dey, C. 2003. Direktinvestitionen in den mittel- und osteuropäischen Beitrittsländern: Rückwirkungen auf den deutschen Arbeitsmarkt? *Wirtschaft im Wandel* 9(4), pp. 98-104.

Elsner, B. & Zimmermann, K.F. 2013. 10 Years After: EU Enlargement, Closed Borders, and Migration to Germany. *IZA Discussion Paper* 7130. Bonn: IZA.

Epstein, R. A. 2014. Overcoming 'Economic Backwardness' in the European Union. *Journal of Common Market Studies* 52(1), pp. 17-34.

Federal Statistical Office 2014. Foreign Trade. Ranking of Germany's trading partners in foreign trade. Wiesbaden: Statistisches Bundesamt, August 20, 2014.

Felsenthal, D. S. & Machover, M. 2001. The Treaty of Nice and qualified majority voting. *Social Choice and Welfare* 18, pp. 431-464.

Galgóczi, B. & Leschke, J. 2014. Post-Enlargement Intra-EU Labour Mobility Under Stress Test. *Intereconomics* 49(3), pp. 152-158.

Kahanec, M. & Zaiceva, A. & Zimmermann, K. F. 2010. Lessons from Migration after EU Enlargement. In: Kahanec, M. & Zimmermann, K. F. (Eds.). *EU Labor Markets After Post-Enlargement Migration.* Heidelberg et al.: Springer, pp. 3-46.

Katzenstein, P. (Ed.) 1987. *Policy and Politics in Germany: the Growth of a Semisovereign State.* Philadelphia: Temple University Press.

Katzenstein, P. J. 1996. Regionalism in Comparative Perspective. *Cooperation and Conflict* 31, pp. 123-159.

Katzenstein, P. J. 1997. United Germany in an Integrating Europe. Peter J. Katzenstein (Ed.). *Tamed Power: Germany in Europe.* Ithaca: Cornell University Press.

Kirsch, W. 2001. Mathematik und politische Macht. Der EU-Gipfel von Nizza und die Machtstrukturen im Europäischen Rat. *DMV-Mitteilungen* 1, pp. 18-21.

Kirsch, W & Langner J. 2011. Invariably Suboptimal: An Attempt to Improve the Voting Rules of the Treaties of Nice and Lisbon. *Journal of Common Market Studies* 49(6), pp. 1317-1338.

Kohl, H. 1991. Solidarität und Bereitschaft zur Verantwortung – Die Rolle Deutschlands in Europa. Vortrag anlässlich der Eröffnung der zweiten Tagung des „Forum für Deutschland" in Berlin. *Bulletin des Presse- und Informationsamts der Bundesregierung* Nr. 33 (22. March 1991).

Łada, A. 2012. The Poles on Polish-German Relations and Germany's Role in Europe. Main conclusions. Online available at: http://isp.org.pl/uploads/filemanager/pdf/Mainconclussionswithpictures2.pdf (last visit: 22 July 2014).

Leech, D. 2002. Designing the voting system for the Council of the European Union. *Public Choice* 113, pp. 437-464.

Meardi, G. & Marginson, P. & Fichter, M. & Frybes, M. & Stanojevic, M. & Tóth, A. 2009. The Complexity of Relocation and the Diversity of Trade Union Responses: Efficiency-oriented Foreign Direct Investment in Central Europe. *European Journal of Industrial Relations* 15(1), pp. 27-47.

Medve-Bálint, Gy. 2014. The Role of the EU in Shaping FDI Flows to East Central Europe. Journal of Common Market Studies 52(1), pp. 35-51.

Ochmann, R. R. 2005. The First EU Eastern Enlargement. Impacts on the German Economy and the Public Perceptions. *Institute for World Economics, Hungarian Academy of Science, Working Papers* 158.

Parkes, R. 2013. How Poland Came to Be a Major EU Power. Strategic Europe. online available: http://carnegieeurope.eu/strategiceurope/?fa=51958 (last visit: 22 July2014).

Paterson W. E. 2005. European policy making: between associated sovereignty and semi-sovereignty. in Green S. & Paterson W. E. (Eds.). *Governance in contemporary Germany.* Cambridge: Cambridge University Press, pp. 261-282.

Paterson, W. E. 2011. The Reluctant Hegemon? Germany Moves Centre Stage in the European Union. *Journal of Common Market Studies* 49, pp. 57-75.

Pond, E. 1992. Germany in the New Europe. *Foreign Affairs* 71(2), pp. 114-130.

Schimmelfennig, F. 2001. The Community Trap: Liberal Norms, Rhetorical Action, and the Eastern Enlargement of the European Union. *International Organization* 55(1), pp. 47-80.

Schuck, A. R. T. & de Vreese, C. H. 2006. Between Risk and Opportunity: News Framing and its Effects on Public Support for EU Enlargement. *European Journal of Communication* 21(5), pp. 5-32.

Sperling J. 2001. Neither Hegemony nor Dominance: Reconsidering German Power in Post Cold-War Europe. *British Journal of Political Science* 31(2), pp. 389-425.

Statistisches Bundesamt 2014. Bevölkerung und Erwerbstätigkeit. Ausländische Bevölkerung Ergebnisse des Ausländerzentralregisters 2013. Wiesbaden: Statistisches Bundesamt, 24. April 2014.

Taylor, P. G. 2008. The End of European Integration: Anti-Europeanism Examined. London: Routledge.

Treaty on European Union 1992. *Official Journal of the European Communities* C 191, pp. 1-112.

Treaty of Nice amending the Treaty on European Union, the Treaties establishing the European Communities and certain related acts 2001. *Official Journal of the European Communities* C80, pp. 1-87.

Więcławski, J. 2010. The Eastern Enlargement of the European Union: Fears, Challenges, and Reality. *Globality Studies Journal* 15, pp. 1-11.

Więcławski, J. 2011. Poland East-Central Europe and the European Union's Policy towards Russia. *International Journal of Humanities and Social Science* 1(4), pp. 23-30.

Wood, St. 2002a. Apprehensive Partners: Germany, Poland and EU Enlargement. *German Politics* 11(1), pp. 97-124.

Wood, St. 2002b. Germany and the Eastern Enlargement of the EU: Political Elites, Public Opinion and Democratic Processes. *Journal of European Integration* (24)1, pp. 23-38.

Wood, St. 2003. Is Eastern Enlargement of the European Union a Beneficial Investment for Germany? *Political Science Quarterly* 118(2), pp. 281-306.

Rescuing the Euro – Consequences for the Future of the Euro and of Europe

Rigmar Osterkamp

1. My main points in our Seoul conference in 2012

In our conference in Seoul, two years ago, I arrived at some conclusions which can be summarized in nine points:

1. The introduction of the Euro was and is a political project. It is intended to make an ever tighter European Union – and peace in Europe – irrevocable.
2. The introduction of the Euro is based on political, not economic reasoning. Most economists in Europe and elsewhere have doubted – and are doubting – whether the Euro or the Euro area can survive when weaker members are exposed to economic and financial shocks that they cannot anymore counter by depreciating their currency.
3. The reason for the doubts is that the Euro area lacks main characteristics of an optimal currency area: mobility of labour, flexible labour markets, similar levels of standard of living, similar degrees of competitiveness, similar labour market and social institutions, symmetric effects of shocks. These characteristics are necessary to make up for the abandoned possibility of exchange rate changes and to make a common monetary policy reasonable.
4. The basis for the – still looming – crisis has been laid by the dramatic equalization of interest rates that followed the (virtual) introduction of the Euro (1995) by fixing the exchange rates irrevocably. Interest rates (mainly in the Southern Euro area countries) [1] declined to the low level of the Northern Euro countries.
5. Demand for (now cheap) credit in Southern countries triggered large capital flows from "North" to "South" and an increase of private, pub-

---

[1] The case of Ireland, however, is different in some respects. I do not go into these differences in this contribution.

lic and bank debt. The credits mainly fuelled a construction boom and the production of non-tradables, less so of tradables.

6. Despite of the "no bail-out" clause in the currency treaties, creditors believed in the safety of their financial investments, i.e. they believed that the Euro area will be held together, whatever it takes. (So far they have been largely right – with the exception of the haircut done to their Greece and Cyprus investments.)

7. These dramatic developments and their crisis potential went largely unnoticed. It was only the global financial crisis, starting in the US in 2007, which laid open the unsustainable financial positions taken by banks and by public and private actors in Southern Euro countries.

8. For stabilizing the Euro area, the Northern Euro countries started comprehensive rescue measures which had mainly the following elements: debt cut, fresh credit, keeping interest rates low, and structural reforms. A debt cut occurred in Greece and Cyprus. However, Greek debt, for example, was only minimally affected by the debt cut due to the continuation of public deficits.

9. The structural reforms were intended to reduce budget deficits, increase competitiveness and to eliminate bad loans from banks' balance sheets.

Now we look at the following questions:

- Which effect have the Euro rescue measures had so far?
- Which additional measures are planned or discussed?
- Which new developments may influence future rescue operations?
- The Euro and Europe – what may happen?

2. Which effect have the Euro rescue measures had so far?

2.1 The positive side of the coin

There are two positive developments so far: First, the Euro area did not shrink. The problem countries Greece, Portugal, Spain and Ireland are still members of the Euro zone. And since January 2014 this year Latvia has joined the Euro zone. Lithuania is scheduled for membership next year. Then all three Baltic countries will be Euro area members. (Chart 1)

Chart 1 Euro zone so far is continuously expanding: 18 Euro countries in 2014

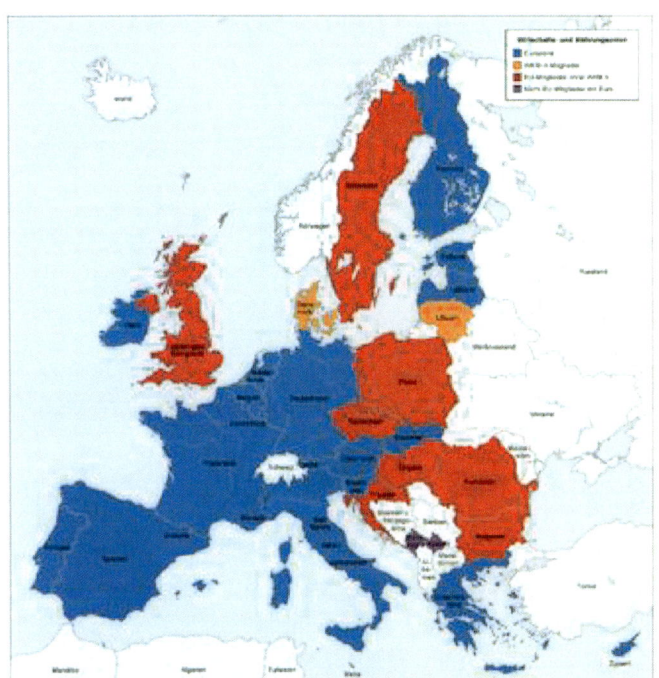

In blue colour: Euro countries; Source: European Commission.

Second, the Euro is still a strong currency. It is only in the first years after the introduction of the Euro in 1995 that the Euro became weaker. Since 2000, the Euro grew in strength and went from 0.82 US$ per 1 Euro to 1,40 US$ where it has more or less stabilized on that level (Chart 2) – not even seriously affected by the global financial crisis.

Chart 2

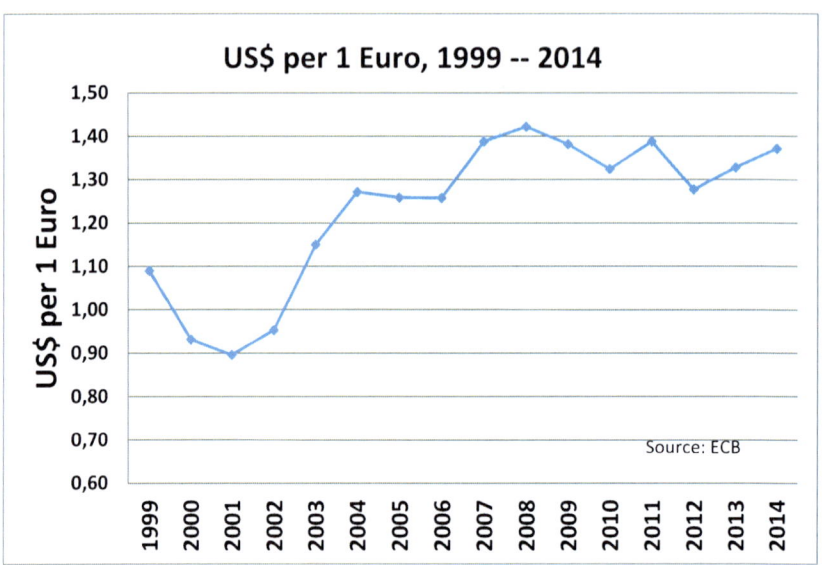

The strength of the Euro can also be seen from its use as an international reserve currency. Between 1999 and 2009, the Euro has considerably gained worldwide importance (from 18% to 28%). Thereafter its use declined slightly to 25% in 2013.[2]

Another positive development is, at least at first glance, that the financial markets in Europe are calm. They have been successfully calmed by some massive ECB operations or by the ECB promising "to do whatever is necessary" for destroying expectations of financial investors of falling prices of debt instruments of Greece and other countries.

Of only mild relief is the improvement of the balance of payments in the problem countries. There is, indeed, a dramatic improvement – but from unsustainable levels. (Chart 3) However, the improvement is mainly due to shrinking imports and not so much due to rising exports. And the reduced imports are mainly a result of low and negative economic growth.

---

2 The US Dollar, while declining in relative importance – from 66% in 2005 to 61% in 2013 –, is still the by far most important reserve currency. Other reserve currencies play only a minor role while the Chinese Renminbi is rapidly expanding its function as the third important reserve currency of the world.

Chart 3

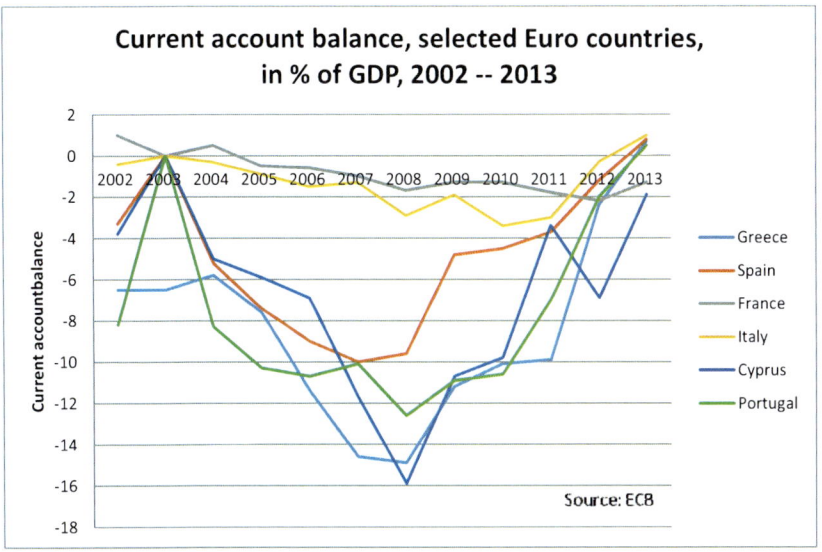

Current account balance, selected Euro countries, in % of GDP, 2002 -- 2013

Source: ECB

2.2 The negative side of the coin

The price for these positive developments is high, particularly for the weak Southern countries. Their problem is to regain lost competitiveness and to restore a viable financial position of the public, the banking and the private sectors – without the possibility of devaluating the currency. This leaves open only one route: the so-called internal devaluation, i.e. prices and wages must be reduced.

It was clear from the outset that this is only possible with a period of low economic growth and a high level of unemployment. However, it has not been expected by most observers that economic growth would become negative, that unemployment would grow into a mass phenomenon and that all this seems to take quite a number of years before a viable situation can be achieved. (Table 1) These developments seriously endanger the so-cietal cohesion of the Southern countries. In Greece and Spain, a quarter of the workforce is unemployed, youth unemployment is even near 50%.

Table 1 Unemployment rates, selected European countries, April 2014

Greece	26.5%	Italy	12.6%
Spain	25.1%	France	10.4%
Croatia	16.8%	Euro Zone	11.7%
Zyprus	16.4%	EU	10.4%
Portugal	14.6%		

Source: Eurostat

During the Euro rescue operations from 2007 until now, public external debt in the Southern periphery countries increased dramatically, in Greece from around 100% of GDP to 170%, in Portugal from 70% to 125%, in Spain from a very low level of 34% to more than 100%. In Greece, the primary budget balance (leaving interest payments out of the picture) was negative since Greece's inception in the Euro zone. It is hoped now that it will become positive in 2014. Total budget balance is of course much more negative due to interest payments – and adds continuously to the existing public debt and the country's external debt.

Another problematic development in the Euro zone is disinflation, as it is sometimes called: the steady decline of the inflation rate to levels which are regarded as too low. Currently the inflation rates stands at 0.7% only, while the target rate is "near to, but not higher than 2%". (Chart 4)

Chart 4 GDP Deflator in Euro countries

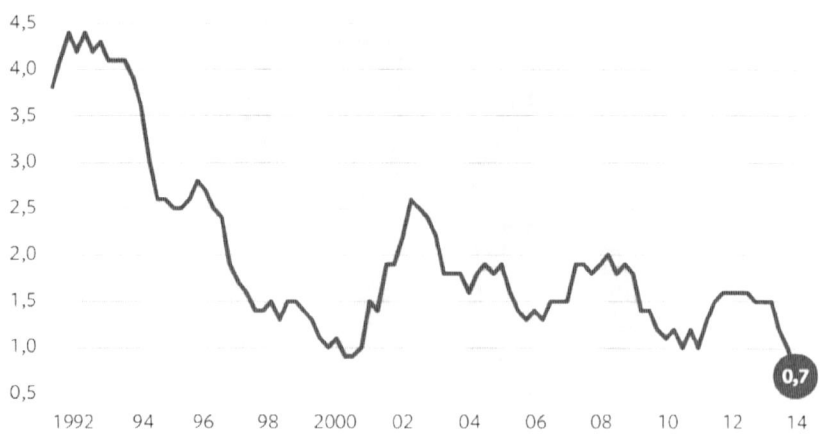

Source: Bloomberg Research

One reason for this development is of course the internal devaluation policy in the Southern problem countries. For the ECB it is practically impossible to implement a monetary policy which is adequate for all members of the Euro zone – a problem which has been seen by many economists even before the introduction of the Euro.

A problem seems to arise also in France. French banks are heavily engaged with credits to the Southern periphery and depend, thus, very much on the success of rescue operations. At the same time, French unemployment is high as is her public debt and deficit, while economic growth is low. France, together with Italy and the Southern problem countries, argues for a redefinition of the stability criteria which are, however, agreed to be applicable to all Euro countries.

More and more doubts are raised in Europe whether austerity is really necessary for regaining international competitiveness, for reducing unemployment and for re-establishing an acceptable level of economic growth. These doubts are in principle fully justified – were it not for the high external and internal debt levels achieved in the past. Unfortunately, the debt levels are partly due to the rescue operations themselves which consist of putting credit after credit on already high debt levels. These high debt levels make it impossible for the problem countries to follow Keynesian recipes of overcoming unemployment by (more) deficit spending.

Some observers even doubt whether there is at all an austerity policy in the problem countries. They argue that public budgets in most of these countries are still in deficit. That is true. But it is a misunderstanding to identify "austerity" with a **public** budget balance only and only with its **level**. Not only public budgets are of relevance. Budget balance of private households and of enterprises is of equal importance. And: not the level of the (aggregate) budget balance – be it a deficit or a surplus – is decisive for a stimulating or dampening effect on the economy. It is rather the **change** of the balance. Only an **increased deficit** (or a reduced surplus) is able to exert a stimulating effect. Unfortunately, this route is practically closed for most countries in the Euro zone. What most countries really did, is to lower the budget deficits of public authorities and of the private sector. And this is, indeed, austerity policy which has been applied also by Greece, for example. (Chart 5) Unfortunately, this policy is unavoidable, though it sharpens current pains.

Chart 5 Shrinking public finance deficits in Greece

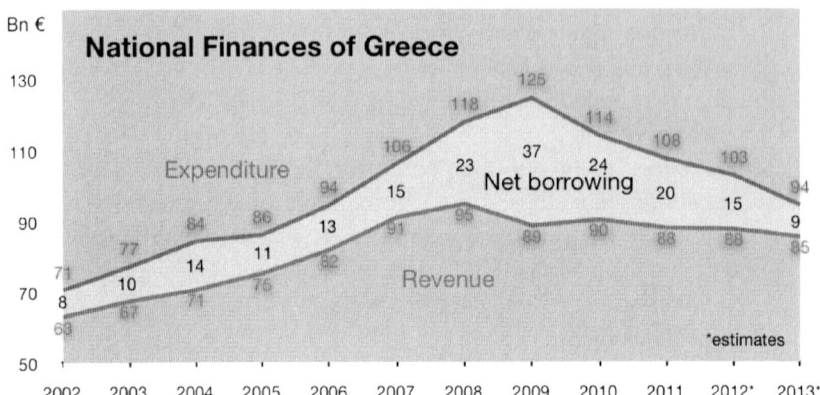

Source: Eurostat

3. Which additional measures are planned or discussed?

It has become increasingly clear that the rules and institutions agreed upon at the introduction of the Euro are not sufficient for weathering external shocks and are not sufficiently respected. Thus, much post-shock repair work has to be done and is being done.

One of these attempts is to establish a "Banking Union" consisting of three parts:

a) A Euro-area-wide central system of bank supervision is to be started end of 2014. This is intended to avoid a national "race to the bottom" with regards to liquidity and safety rules. The problem here is that it is the ECB – and not a specialized institution – which has got the authority to assess liquidity and safety of banks' operations. It may well be that a conflict of interest arises when the ECB had to insist on higher equity capital or lower leverage of a bank – but hesitates to do so because this procedure may endanger ECB's own assets, namely ECB credits previously granted to that bank.

b) A rescue fund (Resolution Fund) will contain (finally) Euro 55 billions. But large banks operating in the Euro area have assets of over Euro 1 trillion. Thus, the rescue fund may be much too small. Moreover, there is still no legal procedure for the liquidation of bankrupt banks.

c) A Euro-area-wide guarantee fund for deposits was also planned – but has been dropped. Some countries, Germany included, were afraid that such a fund would amount to a "transfer union" in which German banks and German taxpayers would eventually bear the costs of other banks' unsafe behavior.

Another attempt is to establish a "Fiscal Union". The content of "Fiscal Union" is much less clear than that of "Banking Union". Some observers consider a Fiscal Union to be one with a centralized fiscal authority, being placed on top of national governments and disposing of own tax revenues. Currently, a Fiscal Union of this sort has no realistic political perspective. In the light of economics it would make sense only when symmetric shocks occur. But so far, most shocks in the Euro area have been asymmetric. So, the centralized fiscal authority had to give money to specific countries in need. But that amounts to a transfer union which is strictly refused by most Northern countries.

A "Fiscal Union" of a much more limited – but not at all low – significance is what has been introduced in 2011, namely the so-called "Sixpack". This is the attempt to strengthen the "Stability and Growth Pact" (SGP) of 1998, three years after fixing the exchange rates of national currencies to the Euro (1995 – the virtual introduction of the Euro) and four years before the introduction of Euro bills and coins (2002). The SGP was set up in order to avoid excessive public budget deficits of Euro member countries. From 2002 onwards – and even before 2002 – the rules of the SGP have been violated in many years by many countries and repeatedly. The required penalty payments have never been paid, not even asked for by the EU Commission. National governments were strong enough – and united enough – to make the EU Commission remain silent, even after repeated violations of the rules.

The "Sixpack" is now meant to make the SGP more effective – more binding and more biting. It consists of the following six elements:

1. *Strengthening of the surveillance of budgetary positions and of economic policies.*
2. *Speeding up and clarifying the implementation of the excessive deficit procedure.*
3. *More effective enforcement of budgetary surveillance in the euro area.*
4. *Defining requirements for budgetary frameworks of the member states.*

5. *Better prevention and correction of macroeconomic imbalances.*
6. *Improving enforcement action to correct excessive macroeconomic imbalances.*

Only future will tell whether the Sixpack rules – as another attempt to make member countries behave in a way that is conducive for a currency union – will achieve their aim.

A powerful rescue institution is the ECB – and not only through its future banking supervision activities but also through its *normal* monetary policy. However, it is not so normal because the ECB's buying of government bonds is not performed in a general manner, i.e. equally affecting all Euro countries, but it is country-specific. The ECB argues that this procedure is necessary to make up for failures of the monetary policy transmission mechanism. But it relieves interest pressure particularly from budget deficit countries. Thus, it can be regarded as fiscal policy and as a hidden bail-out – which is forbidden by the Euro treaties for the ECB to do.

It would be of great help for the problem countries and for the cohesion of the Euro zone if the economically stronger countries – like Germany, the Netherlands or Finland – would increase their inflation rate. This would lower the necessary internal devaluation, i.e. deflation, in the problem countries. But this is easier demanded than realized. Germany, for example, is since some years on the opposite course by reducing step by step her public deficits. This is austerity policy, though in a mild and slow form. But it is not, of course, of help for the problem countries. Unfortunately, for Germany this policy is difficult to avoid. German public debt is with around 80% already much beyond the upper target ceiling of 60% and must be reduced. A conscious inflationary policy could only be initiated by the government through an increase of salaries of government employees. This would be rather effective in terms of inflation because all other segments of the labour market would follow suit. But it would be the end of the policy of reducing the public debt level.

Old ideas, not implemented and highly controversial, concern the introduction of "Euro Bonds" and of a EU-wide unemployment insurance.

4. Which new developments may influence future rescue operations?

A new, and at the same time old development is that deficit countries express doubts about the usefulness and applicability of the general rules "to their special case". In June this year, high ranking politicians of Southern and Northern (!) countries came to the conclusion that the SGP with its clarification in form of the Sixpack is too strict and not adequate to the specific situation of their country. If being outside of a currency union, deficit countries had to accept the bitter medicine of a devaluation. Being inside, they try to avoid the bitter medicine of fiscal prudence. The Six-pack is only three years old – and already put into question.

Another new development is a ruling of the German Constitutional Court about the planned "Outright Monetary Transaction" (OMT) pro-gram of the ECB. The OMT program is openly (and not in a hidden way) directed to help deficit countries finance their deficits. So far, no opera-tions within that program have been conducted. The ruling of the German court puts great doubts on the legality of that program, given the "no-bail-out clause" of the EU treaties. However, the German court has no power over a European institution like the ECB. It could only force the German Central Bank, being part of the ECB system, to decline any participation in the conduct of this program. So far, the court has limited itself to ex-press doubts about the legality of the OMT program – and to remit the case to the European Constitutional Court.

A third new (though, not so new) development is the growing critical stance of most parties in Britain (not a Euro zone member) towards the EU Commission, its new president and the EU generally.

A final new development is the recent election to the European Parlia-ment. A strong minority of the seats has been won by parties who share at least several of the following critical views:

- The EU has been extended too quickly to more members and to the wrong members.
- The EU Commission acts in matters which should be better settled by member countries themselves, for example labour standards, hospital standards, education standards and even standards governing the size and forms of cucumber.
- The EU Commission does not act sufficiently in matters which should be better dealt with on an EU level, for example energy and defense.
- The Euro is a dubious blessing for economically weak countries. There should be a structured and agreed-upon way of leaving the Euro zone – and of returning to the Euro after devaluation.

The European Parliament's competencies are rather limited and cannot stand a comparison with the rights of a national parliament of a democratic country. But it remains to be seen what impact the new critical minority in the EU Parliament will be able to exert on the actions of the EU Commission and on the national governments. It is the latter – and not the Parliament – which define the further development of Europe.

5. The Euro and Europe – what may happen?

For the Euro to have a real future some important changes have to be made. Some observers and most politicians see these important changes as having being already done or at least agreed upon. This is the Banking Union, the Fiscal Union and an ever more powerful ECB. Some other observers and most economists, the present author included, regard other and more radical moves as necessary to prevent an eventual failure of the whole Euro project.

- In order to make the existing – but toothless – "no- bail-out" clause effective, there should be a bankruptcy procedure for Euro area governments. The respective rules in the US could serve as a role model.
- Countries must be able to leave the Euro zone without leaving the European Union – and without giving up the duty free access to the other EU member countries.
- There also must be a bankruptcy procedure for banks.
- Banks must become restructured in order to reduce their political leverage and moral hazard behavior.

Most probably, such new developments will have difficulties to appear. Instead, a continuation of the current muddling-through policies is more probable. This will include the repeated application of the rule of rule-breaking: "necessity knows no law" – already applied several times by Euro member governments and by the ECB. Unfortunately, high unemployment in many countries and low interest rates for all Euro zone countries will continue for quite a number of years to cause production and welfare losses for most EU member countries.

In my view, the Euro as a currency of worldwide relevance and used by important countries is not at stake. What is at stake is the Euro area in its current composition. It may need only a marginal change of the political landscape in one of the problem countries that it comes to a majority that favors an exit from the Euro. This would be seen by some politicians in Europe as a tragedy. In my view, however, it would not endanger but would ensure and stabilize what is most important: the continuation of the European peace project.

Literature

Baldwin, R., Ch. Wyplosz (2004), *The Economics of European Integration.* New York: McGraw

Hill.

Bernholz, P. (2012), "The current account deficits of the GIPS countries and their target deficits at the ECB", *CESifo Forum*, January.

Blankart, Ch. (2012), "The Euro in 2084", *CESifo Forum*, January.

Buiter, W.H., Rahbari, E. (2011), "The future of the euro area: Fiscal union, break-up or

blundering? Towards a you-break-it, you-own-it Europe", *Citi Group Research Paper.*

Condogn, T. (1998), "A Maoist leap forward? The single currency and European political union",

The Selsdon Group Policy Paper.

European Central Bank (2012), *The international role of the euro*, (July); Frankfurt a.M.: ECB.

European Economic Advisory Group (EEAG), (2011), *The EEAG Report on the European*

Economy, Munich: CESifo.

Friedman, M. (1997), "Why Europe can't afford the euro", *The Times* (19 September).

Issing, O. (2011), "Slithering to the wrong kind of union", *Financial Times* (8 August).

Mundell, R. A. (1961), "A Theory of Optimum Currency Areas", *American Economic Review*

51 (4): 657–665.

Sinn, H.-W. (2014), *The Euro Trap: On Bursting Bubbles, Budgets and Beliefs*, Oxford University Press.

Sinn, II.-W. (2010), *Casino Capitalism: How the Financial Crisis Came About and What*

Needs to be Done Now, Oxford University Press. In Korean language: Seoul: Ecopia (translated by Professor Hun Dae Lee).

Sinn, H.-W. (2010), "Rescuing Europe", *CESifo Forum*, Special Issue, #11, August.

The International Financial Crisis and its Effects on the World Economy and the Economic Theory

Heinz Steinmüller and Jona van Laak

This essay wants to trace the International Financial Crisis since 2008 and its effects on the World Economy. The main interest is to show, whether politics, the economy and the society have learned from the crisis and if the scientific economic approach can still correspond to reality. The German philosopher Gottfried Wilhelm Hegel noted so aptly in the 19th century, that each philosophy is a philosophy of its time. Therefore, it must be questioned, whether our current economic theory can still answer the economic questions of the 21st century.

1. Development of the World Economy since 2008

The international financial crisis dealt a blow to the world economy in 2008 and 2009. The yearly growth rate of the world GDP went into the negative and the indicators for the world economic climate fell drastically. Up to 2013 the economic growth of the emerging economies was more crucial for the growth of the world economy than that of the industrialized countries. In addition to a number of structural problems, this development results from an increasing difficulty in refinancing government debt.[1] This holds for countries such as India, Indonesia, Brazil or Argentina. The bankruptcy of Argentina in August of 2014 is the tip of an economic policy of incurring debt which had been supported by the voters for a long time. The Argentine people will now have to pay a heavy price for this credit-based prosperity of the last decades. They will have to live with strong restrictions in the social sector and the real economy.[2]

---

1 Cfr. CESifo (2014a): 3
2 Cfr. Straubhaar (2014)

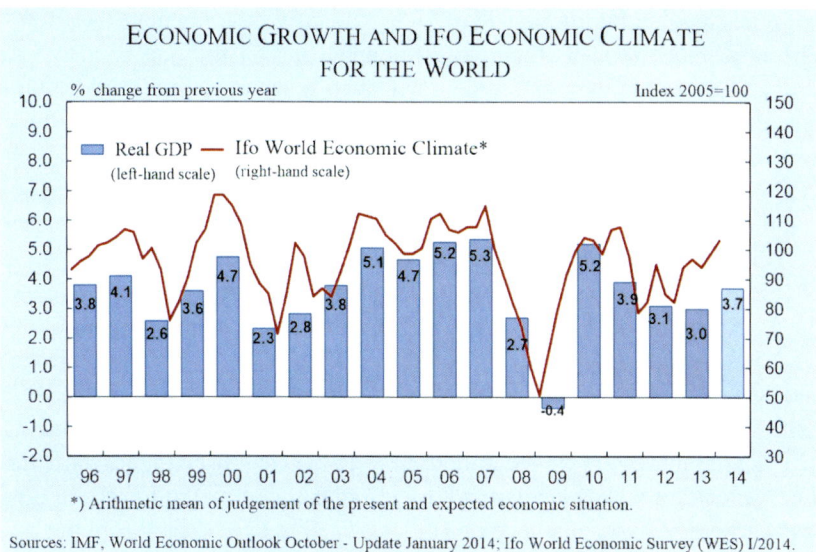

ECONOMIC GROWTH AND IFO ECONOMIC CLIMATE
FOR THE WORLD

*) Arithmetic mean of judgement of the present and expected economic situation.

Sources: IMF, World Economic Outlook October - Update January 2014; Ifo World Economic Survey (WES) I/2014.

In the current situation, there are mainly the industrialized countries of North America and Western Europe which exert positive effects on the world economy: an economic growth which is accompanied by expansive monetary policies, for example in the USA, the UK or the Eurozone. The growth rate of the world production is estimated at around three per cent for 2014 and 2015, that of the world trade at below five per cent. It has to be considered, however, that the influence of the world trade on the world economy has become very weak in the last few years which can be explained by protectionist measures and falling export efforts in the Eurozone.[3] Nevertheless, many experts predict an increase in investment activity due to the stable growth of world trade. OECD studies remain subdued, listing the fragile world economy, the dependence of Japan and Europe on cheap money and the unstable emerging economies which are very responsive to fluctuations in the financial market.[4]

The future development of economic growth after 2015 is forecast as quite restrained by some experts. So, it is argued that the weak economies of the Eurozone will still require years, in order to regain the lost economic growth of the last years. The real GDP of the Eurozone will reach the

3 Cfr. CESifo (2014b): 3; ECB (2014): 2
4 Cfr. Rist (2014)

pre-crisis level not until the end of 2015, so is the assessment of the ECB.[5] The implementation of *Abenomics* in Japan has on the one hand led to strong increases in exports on the other hand it has made the import of oil much more expensive and has therefore triggered negative effects on trade and the current accounts. The economic boom lacks a dynamic labour market, young professionals and solid public spending in order to be successful in the long term.[6]

After a decline from 2007 to 2009 the climate indicator has risen since 2010; it is, how-ever, still below its long term average for Europe. Nevertheless, there are still a number of negative aspects. Unemployment in the USA is still high, in the GIIPS – states (i.e. Greece, Italy, Ireland, Portugal and Spain) it is dramatic: youth unemployment being around 50 %. This high unemployment rate in Europe has caused anti-European movements in crisis countries like Greece and Italy and it has brought forward the emergence of a *lost generation* who feels abandoned by the European policy. These developments have been recognized much too late from the political side.[7] Structural problems in the banking sector can be listed as a second aspect. In spite of a policy of very low interest rates, which led to a permanent increase in money supply in the Eurozone, lending to companies and private banks is still limited.[8]

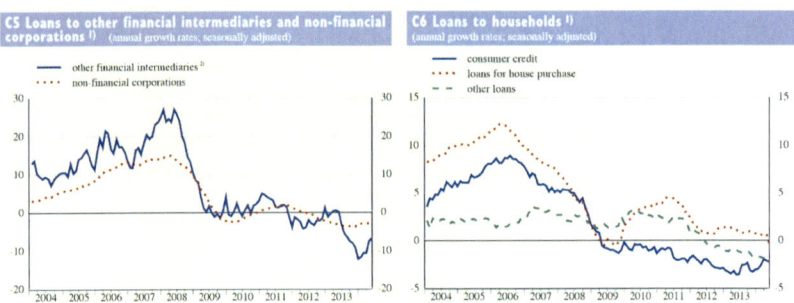

This limits credits for investment activities and restricts economic growth.

---

5 Cfr. ECB (2014a): 1, 4
6 Cfr. Ruzicic (2014)
7 Cfr. Finkenkeller (2013); Hampel (2014)
8 Cfr. CESifo (2014b): 17ff;

2. Regional Economic Outlook

East Asian countries, especially China, responded to the crisis with a large increase in government demand. This policy led to a quick success. In 2010 growth had again exceeded the eight per cent mark. Up to 2016 growth is estimated to slow to a sustainable level of around seven per cent. The outlook depends on the development of financing conditions, the global demand for imports and the political crisis in Thailand.[9] Whereas the economic growth in India, Sri Lanka and the Philippines is slowly increasing, the speed of Chinese growth has decreased. China currently has excess capacities in the industrial sector and in housing. Economic growth in Japan is developing attenuated. Despite the expansionary monetary policy and devaluation of the yen no significant increase in exports could be achieved.[10]

Latin America has been hit hard by the crisis, mainly due to the decrease in investment activity. The high economic growth from 2003 to 2008, well over 4 per cent and the good refinancing conditions have helped to reduce poverty and renovate government budgets. The economic slump since 2008 is due to the low levels of foreign investment, to problems in refinancing and to structural deficits. These problems have been accompanied by a clearly increasing inflation, e.g. in Venezuela. The outlook of the World Bank estimates a regional growth from 1.9 per cent in 2014 up to over 3 per cent in 2016.[11] However, strong regional differences can be discerned. While the economy of Mexico or the Dominican Republic is gaining strength, Argentina and Venezuela remain weak. Similar regional differences can be shown in Africa, with extreme differences in the development level of the economies. In general, it can be stated that there are no common economic trends and that the economic situation is currently "assessed as unfavourable"[12] in most African countries.

The transformation process in the Soviet Union had led to a serious economic slump in the 1990s. Only in 2007, Russia's GDP reached again the 1989 level. But this should not obscure the fact that this GDP level was due to high oil and gas exports. Russia is still confronted with significant structural weaknesses. Therefore, it was hit in the 2008 financial cri-

---

9 Cfr. WB (2014a):35
10 CESifo (2014b): 10, 11, 40
11 Cfr. WB (2014b): 53
12 Cfr. CESifo (2014b): 18

sis by credit crunches and the resulting reduction of investment activity, whereas the Russian banking system could be stabilized quickly by governmental intervention.[13] The strong decline of the oil price in 2009 led to a sharp fall in the real economy. Out of this severe recession Russia managed to recover just very slowly in the following years. Up to date, the conditions for economic growth are very unfavourable in all states of the former Soviet Union, resulting from high administrative restrictions that prevent foreign companies from capital investment.[14] The political instability in the Ukraine and the economic sanctions against Russia will result in further negative effects on the economy.

The USA has become the driving force in the current economic upturn of the world economy, with a growth of GDP estimated at about 3 per cent in 2015. This recovery is based on increasing consumer confidence, on rising employment and rising wealth and income. This development caused increasing state revenues which have led, combined with the government's consolidation-policy in the last two years, to a significant reduction of the budget deficit. The uncertainties of the monetary policy of the Fed have been reduced and the purchase of fixed-income securities has declined. Experts expect an increase in interest rates by the Fed in mid-2015.[15]

Europe, as well, is on the road to recovery from the long period of recession. The confidence of market participants has increased, labour markets and shares could mainly be stabilized. The declining concern about the euro has led to rising investment and consumption activities.[16] However, there are critical factors: the situation of the banks, the high debt ratios and financing costs that arise because the nominal interest rate is well above the rate of inflation in some countries.[17] In Eastern Europe the recovery is much more subdued as compared to Western Europe.

3. The limits of conventional economic theories

What we have come to call the International Financial Crisis is actually a cascade of different and interdependent crises:

---

13 Cfr. Grigorjew (2008): 1-5
14 Cfr. CESifo (2014a): 8
15 Cfr. CESifo (2014a): 8; CESifo (2014b): 6f
16 Cfr. CESifo (2014b): 1, 4
17 Cfr. Ibd., 6f

- housing-bubble (subprime credit or real estate crisis)
- banking and insurance crisis
- international financial crisis proper
- economic crisis (recession / depression)
- public debt crisis
- EURO – crisis
- social crisis
- political crisis

Having said this, it is evident that an isolated scientific economic approach does no longer make sense. Isolated means that the above series of problems are being addressed by economics, by sociology, by political science and other sciences separately. Let us quote Thomas Piketty who writes in his book *Capital in the Twenty-First Century:* "The truth is that economics should never have sought to divorce itself from the other social sciences"[18]. By the way, it is this interdisciplinary approach which is adopted by the HfP in its academic teaching – the HfP which we are supposed to call now *Bavarian School of Public Policy.*

Following the assessment of Andrew Haldane, executive director at the Bank of England, the financial crisis has made it unmistakably clear, that the foundations of economics must not be considered as being stable.[19] These foundations include the market model of the invisible hand and all the well-known theorems of modern economics. Haldane rightly noted that unlimited self-interest, greed and boundless competition in the financial sector have actually harmed the society. In the situation of crisis people do not longer act rationally such as would be expected by the standard economic models. Haldane is thus one of the most prominent representatives of a new economic thinking which demands a renewal of the economic discipline.

The end of the Bretton Woods system and the associated detachment of the currencies from the gold standard in the 1970s have led to a divergence of the real economy and the financial markets. The different development dynamics of these markets have resulted in the problem that the common economic theory could not follow up with these requirements. Today's economic theory wrongly assumes that financial markets can be analysed with a purely mathematical and calculative science, completely

---

18 Piketty (2014): 32
19 Cfr. Uhlig (2014a)

detached from anthropological and psychological factors.[20] In a highly regarded contribution in the *Süddeutsche Zeitung*, Silja Graupe, Professor of Economics in *Bernkastel-Cues*, identified three causes for the deficiencies of the economic theory: its one-sidedness, its distance to reality and its negative impact on reality.[21] The last cause is decisive – economic theory does not only hinder troubleshooting but can even contribute to the emergence of problems. The Harvard economist Alberto Alesi summarized in June 2014 that the loss of confidence of the people in economics during the financial and economic crisis was mainly caused by the fact that people felt not being understood by economics. This feeling was accompanied by experts who pretended to know more than they actually did and by the fact that the economies were hit by the crisis totally unprepared. This resulted in the situation that people had no confidence in the economic science at a time where this confidence was urgently needed.[22]

The intensification of liberal economic thinking since the 1970s has on the one hand led to a reduction of trade obstructions and has contributed to a better exploitation of the market potential but on the other hand produced a variety of problems which we are facing today. But what is the term free-market philosophy supposed to be and what would be the results? Today's free market theory has degenerated into a model in the sense of *l'art pour l'art* that means economists sitting in ivory towers, playing with glass beads and working for their own sake. If economists no longer wish to degenerate themselves as being meaningless for reality, if they want to meet their responsibility for society they have to face reality. That means they have to develop models which allow a normative application and do not correspond to the interests of the big players but serve the economy as a whole. Applying obsolete models with more and more growth, with cheap labour or cheap energy (fracking) are doomed to fail. This is only a matter of time.

Another crucial point is the role of the scientific elite. It can be wonderfully exemplified by Thomas Piketty. Piketty's recent publication *The capital* has led to an outcry in society and science and this is less due to the fact that he has re-invented the wheel but that, for the first time, in a long period, a loud voice from the academic field of economics has risen to speak. Byung-Chul Han has detected in an essay in the *Süddeutsche*

---

20 Cfr. Von Braun, Platow (2014): 32
21 Cfr. Graupe (2014)
22 Cfr. Alesina (2014)

Zeitung[23] that today's capitalism has made revolutions impossible and it can be added that any critique on capitalism is not regarded as a scientific endeavour but rather a political matter. Capitalism has reached such a powerful position that questioning its inherent logic is regarded as questioning the political system as a whole and that therefore a smell of anti-democratic thinking adheres to any criticism on capitalism. For this reason, critical economic theory has to fight for its place in the social debate again. It has to fight for its scientific status. This is the duty of new economic theorists and especially of the scientific elite. Otherwise economics is up to degenerate to the role it has played under communism – a servant of politics.

4. The crisis

Having a closer look at the above cascade of crises another factor becomes evident. There are actually two crises. The first one which started with the housing-bubble in the USA affected in its consequences the world economy as a whole. The second one is due to the inherent weaknesses of the European Currency Union, i.e. of the EURO.[24] Whereas the world economy is gradually returning to normal – with some exceptions of course – many countries of EURO-land are still in severe trouble. Undoubtedly, Germany is

an exemption here. We will not give an analysis of the economic situation in different countries but focus on more general topics.

It might be helpful to briefly analyse the reasons and deficiencies which led to this disaster which we have come to call the Great Recession. It is these deficiencies which shaped the world economy during the last couple of years and which we have to bear in mind if we are prepared to learn from history. It is our intention to show that fundamental principles of the free-market concept were hurt and that this, actually, is one of the main reasons for the disaster.

Let us look first at the housing-bubble: low interest rates and an unregulated fierce competition among creditors resulted in subprime credits which went sour when interest rates rose in 2007. Individual rational be-

---

23 Han (2014)
24 Cfr. Uhlig (2014c)

haviour to make the American Dream of an own house come true plus *destructive competition* led into a disaster.

Back in the late nineties leading American banks had developed so-called Collateralized Debt Obligations (CDOs): a bundle of often mortgage - backed securities; the contents of such bundles were rarely known. Consequence: a *lack of transparency* at least on the buyer's side. There was asymmetric information. This lack of information was furthermore increased by insuring those CDOs using Credit Default Swaps (CDSs) and dumping them in so-called conduits on Cayman Islands or even Ireland.

Thus, risk was separated from credit and traded separately - as a rule OTC (over the counter) and not on the regular stock exchange. The rating agencies (Moody's, Fitch, Standard and Poor's) played an ambivalent role in this context. They concentrated on assessing individual risks and were not able to take cumulative risk into account – i.e. the subsequent domino effect due to *risk - shifting*.

5. Banking Crisis

The banking crisis started when Lehman Brothers went bankrupt in mid September 2008 and were not rescued. This was clearly in line with the rationale of a free - market economy which is that inefficient, incompetent and bankrupt enterprises should leave the market – according to Joseph Schumpeter's concept of *creative destruction*. Only more than 100 banks, however, went bankrupt – not the 11,000 during the Great Depression – why?

It was feared that the whole financial system would collapse. An investment banker told us: „The turmoil after not having rescued Lehman Brothers was good for us. It showed the world that there was no alternative to saving us – whatever might happen. Our survival is the prerequisite of the survival of the financial system as a whole. We are too big to fail." This is, however, a clear violation of the free – market principle which requests not to have such a *one-sided concentration of power*. According to the latest studies of the IMF this *too important to fail-policy* will particularly burden the taxpayers. The annual subsidy costs for system-relevant banks are estimated in the USA at 70 billion USD and in the Eurozone at 90 to

100 billion USD.[25] These high subsidies invite the big banks to increased risk-taking – the states will pay anyway. This leads to an unacceptable advantage in competition.

The next step in the above cascade was the financial crisis proper. Due to the intransparency concerning the financial stability of individual banks and their interdependencies with other banks nobody trusted anybody. A credit crunch and profound pessimism regarding the further economic development were the consequence. Finally, it came to a depression. The annual loss in GDP was 5 per cent in Germany in 2009, exports fell by 15 per cent, public debt increased dramatically.

Again, in contrast to the principles of a liberal market national states *bailed out banks and insurance companies* and, in addition, launched Keynesian programmes of deficit-spending. Most severely hit was the economy of the so-called GIIPS-states (i.e. Greece, Ireland, Italy, Portugal, Spain). They are all members of the European Currency Union – of EURO-land. Thus, not only the GIIPS-states came into trouble but the EURO as well. The huge differences in terms of competitiveness between, for example, Germany, the Netherlands, Luxemburg on the one hand and the GIIPS-states on the other would have required some *degree of regulation* and devaluation in these countries. But since all 18 countries have the EURO a selective devaluation in the GIIPS-countries is not possible. Free-market (or call it neoliberal) economics would require an internal devaluation, a reduction in public expenditure and substantial reforms. This is in many cases being only reluctantly done – if at all. To prevent future identity-crises in the EU, it would now be necessary to start a discussion about the future of the EU as a transfer union. The objectives of the economic and monetary policy of the EU are not being sufficiently discussed. The establishment of the bank union has opened the back door towards a transfer union. An analysis of how these developments might affect the individual states is therefore overdue[26] – it is the prerequisite to avoid future economic and identity crises.

---

25 Cfr. IMF (2014): 118
26 Alesina (2014)

6. The need for reforms

Substantial reforms are fervently opposed by the voters. And it is not exaggerated to speak of a social crisis in some countries: people losing their homes, being unemployed, living on food banks, rioting and burning cars which all in all leads to a political crisis here and there as well. So, a further increase in public debt seems to be considered as a way out. We are buying time to give leeway to our hopes for possible reforms.

Let us focus now on two aspects which will influence or even shape the world economy furthermore. The first one is the monetary strategy adopted by the Fed, the Bank of England and of Japan and in the meantime by the ECB as well. The Fed has learned from the disastrous mistake made during the Great Depression after 1929. This was to reduce the quantity of money in the USA by 30%. So, in order not to make such a mistake again the quantity of money was increased after the crashes of 1987 and 2001 / 2002. After the Lehman Brothers debacle the quantity was increased in the USA alone by 5 trillion USD. This quantitative easing (QE) is still in practice. The purpose of this strategy is to *bail out*, above all, banks and states. This strategy has resulted in a dramatic reduction in interest rates. Needless to say, that this again is in contrast to the neoliberal market philosophy where a variation of the interest rate is primarily an instrument to *guarantee price stability*. Additionally, the very low interest rates and the high level of stock prices have seduced many financial experts to think that the danger is over. To consider these signals without the circumstances in which they are embedded is a good example of the gap between markets and reality.[27] What about the institutional incapacity or the extremely high level of debts? The Swiss business editor Werner Grundlehner compared the guarantee of low interest rates of central banks as being as reliable with five-year plans in the former communist countries. From his point of view, a guarantee that interest rates will be kept that low should be met with distrust. Central banks might not be able to keep interest rates that artificially low in the next years.[28]

Near zero interest rates prohibit that zombie banks and states fail and it will reduce their cost of financing their debt. But low interest rates are to the disadvantage of savers and their retirement planning. The thereby in-

---

27 Cfr. Uhlig (2014c)
28 Cfr. Grundlehner (2014)

tended investment boom is not in sight and – if so – a misallocation of funds is probable. In addition, one gets the impression that central banks are well-nigh at their wits' end. What strategy should be applied in future crises if there are no more options for interest rate cuts and if the monetary policy options of the ECB are already exhausted in the current situation? The Fed is currently in a precarious situation because the abundance of liquidity has made it nearly impossible to control the prime rate in order to withdraw liquidity. Increasing the deposit rates of the Fed would on the other hand stress the financial system and prevent money market funds from investment. On the side of the Fed it is therefore an aim to prevent an increase of long-term interest rates which could endanger the economic development.[29] This means, however, that the end of the expansionary monetary policy is not in sight yet. Furthermore, think of the negative effects on the cost of public debt when interest rates should be increased one time. In contrast to expectations of 2013, interest rates have even declined in the first half of 2014 again, i.e. government bond rates in euro countries and the USA have partly fallen up to 1 per cent. An increase of the artificially low interest rates could be a danger for the economy if, as a consequence, investors buy bonds rather than shares.[30]

Closely linked with the low interest rate policy is the phenomenon of an extreme excess liquidity which we currently have in Europe. Following the estimation of some experts, the situation in Europe can be compared with the situation in Japan in the 1990s. The economic growth has remained below expectations in the first quarter of 2014, with Germany as an exception. The slow economic growth is mainly due to structural problems. There is a risk of a Japanisation of Europe that means a "combination of a secular stagnation and deflationary trends"[31]. Further parallels between Europe today and Japan in the 1990s are the strong currency, the zombie banks (*too big to fail*) and trade surpluses. Although, there are significant differences in the response to government subsidies or transfer payments. The monetary policy with extremely low interest rates and high liquidity has also contributed to the aggregation of significant high debt

---

29 Cfr. Eisenring (2014)
30 Cfr. Schäfer (2014)
31 Uhlig (2014b) („Kombination einer säkularen Stagnation und eines deflationären Trends")

levels.[32] According to studies by the Bank for International Settlements[33], most of the financial institutions are characterized by high debt levels. Especially European banks have big debt overhangs in their balance sheets. The majority of rating agencies expect that the pressure on bank earnings and balance sheets will remain high, and that in a crisis the states will continue to support banks.[34] In addition, the ECB is considering to buy Asset Backed Securities (ABS).

The second aspect we would like to focus on is *power*. Neither classical nor neoliberal economics deal extensively with power. In a free-market economy the state is not welcome as a *regulating authority*. Remember – deregulation was the motto and there was a race to the bottom for deregulating the financial markets from New York to London and Frankfort, and a number of other places – many of them off-shore.

7. The supremacy of the financial market

And, there are powerful instruments at work: such as derivates, high-speed trading, leveraging, OTC transactions. The volume of trade on the financial markets is gigantic: per year 10 times the world GDP in derivates, 15 times in foreign exchange. Only 2.5 % have real transactions as a background, the rest is speculation which in this case is close to betting. This reflects the enormous power *of* the financial markets. In addition, there are protagonists which have power *over* the markets: investment funds, hedge funds, pension funds, state funds, near-banks and not to forget lobbies. – So, there is an arm behind the invisible hand of the market. An arm that even doesn't hesitate to intervene in scientific teaching.

Nowadays, the guideline for university teaching in economics in Germany and abroad is – more or less – the neoliberal approach. Above all, it has become the guideline for global economic policy, as well. Deregulation was the mantra of Ronald Reagan and Margaret Thatcher. Very often this neoliberal policy, based on neoliberal economics, is held responsible for the mess we are in. The common reaction being: economists should look for a new theoretical approach – a reset of their economic theory as pointed out above.

---

32 Cfr. ib.
33 Cfr. BIS (2014)
34 Cfr. Ferber (2014)

The point we have made in this paper is, however, that the basic rules of this neoliberal approach – call it the rules of free market economics – have been disobeyed and violently hurt. They are:

1. non-destructive competition
2. transparency
3. no risk-shifting and bailing-out
4. absence of one-sided power
5. a necessary degree of regulation
6. monetary policy only to guarantee price stability.
7. morals and good governance

It is the disobedience of these rules which led to the problems we have and the disaster we are in. So, the consequence is not to ask for a new economic theory. The consequence is rather to insist on the rules of traditional neoliberal economics to be implemented.

CHARTS

Chart 1: CESifo (2014a): 3
Chart 2: ECB (2014b): 129 (S 14)

REFERENCES

Alesina, Alberto (2014): Wie Staaten sparen sollten (How States should save money), Interview in: *NZZ* (03/06/2014), 9

BIS (Bank for International Settlements) (2014): 84th Annual Report, Basel, http://www.bis.org/publ/arpdf/ar2014_ec.pdf (Stand 02/09/2014)

CESifo (2014a): World Economy Survey, Munich

CESifo (2014b): ifo Schnelldienst. Gemeinschaftsdiagnose Frühjahr 2014, Nr. 8/2014, Munich

ECB (European Central Bank) (2014a): Von Experten der EZB erstellte Gesamtwirtschaftliche Projektionen für das Euro-Währungsgebiet vom März 2014 (macroeconomic projections for the euro area, created by ECB experts in March 2014), Frankfurt am Main

ECB (2014b): Monthly Bulletin Juli 2014, Frankfurt am Main, http://www.ecb.europa.eu/pub/pdf/mobu/mb201407en.pdf (Stand 07/09/2014)

Eisenring, Cristoph (2014): Riesige Fed-Bilanz als Bürde (huge balance of the Fed as a burden), in: *NZZ* (18/06/2014), 11

Finkenkeller, Karin (2013): Europas später Kampf gegen die Jugendarbeitslosigkeit (Europes late fight against youth unemployment), in: *zeit-online.de* (12/11/2013), http://www.zeit.de/wirtschaft/2013-11/jugendarbeitslosigkeit-europa (Stand 26/08/2014)

Ferber, Michael (2014): Aufgeblähtes EU-Bankensystem (The bloated banking system of Europe), in: *NZZ* (03/07/2014), 12

German Council of Economic Experts (2011): Annual Report 2011/12, Wiesbaden, http://www.sachverstaendigenrat-wirtschaft.de/fileadmin/dateiablage/Sonstiges/chapter_four_2011.pdf (Stand 26/086/2014)

Graupe, Silja (2014): Wider der Monokultur (against the monuculture), in: *SZ* (16/06/2014), 16

Grigorjew, Leonid (2008): Globale Finanzkrise 2008 und Wirtschaft Russlands (global financial crisis 2008 and the economy of russia), Moskau, http://library.fes.de/pdf-files/bueros/moskau/05933.pdf (Stand 07/09/2014)

Grundlehner, Werner (2014): Entkoppelte Zinsen (decoupled interest), in: NZZ (25/03/2014), 11

Hampel, Lea (2014): Herr Hartz hat einen Plan. Jugendarbeitslosigkeit in Europa (Mr. Hartz has a plan. Youth unemployment in Europe), in: *süddeutsche.de* (23/06/2014), http://www.sueddeutsche.de/wirtschaft/jugendarbeitslosigkeit-in-europa-herr-hartz-hat-einen-plan-1.2012121 (Stand 03/08/2014)

Han, Byung-Chul (2014): Warum heute keine Revolution möglich ist (Why revolution is impossible today), in: *süddeutsche.de* (02/09/2014), http://www.sueddeutsche.de/politik/neoliberales-herrschaftssystem-warum-heute-keine-revolution-moeglich-ist-1.2110256 (Stand 07/09/2014)

IMF (International Monetary Fund) (2014): Global Financial Stability Report (04/2014), Washington

Piketty, Thomas (2014): Capital in the Twenty-First Century, Cambridge

Rist, Manfred (2014): Am Tropf des billigen Geldes (On the drip of cheap money), in: *NZZ* (13/03/2014), 9

Ruzicic, Nicole Rütti (2014): Kein solides Fundament in Europa und Japan (no solide basis in Europe and Japan), in: *NZZ* (27/03/2014), 15

Schäfer, Michael (2014): Erhöhte Wachsamkeit ist nötig (increased vigilance is needed), in: *NZZ* (20/05/2014), 11

Straubhaar, Thomas (2014): Argentinien wird noch lange nicht untergehen (Argentina will not fail), in: *welt.de* (07/08/2014), http://www.welt.de/wirtschaft/article130983868/Argentinien-wird-noch-lange-nicht-untergehen.html (Stand 08/08/2014)

Uhlig, Andreas (2014a): Hinterfragte Relevanz der Ökonomie (the challenged relevance of economics), in: *NZZ* (29/04/2014), 14

Uhlig, Andreas (2014b): Die drohende Japanisierung Europas (the impending Japanization of Europe), in: *NZZ* (20/05/2014), 15

Uhlig Andreas (2014c): Die Kluft zwischen Markt und Realität (the gap between the market and reality), in: *NZZ* (17/06/2014), 14

Von Braun, Christina und Platow Alfred (2014): Was das Geld wert ist (about the value of money), Interview in: *chrismon* (07/2014), 30-33

WB (World Bank) (2014a): Global economic prospects. East Asia and the Pacific, http://www.worldbank.org/content/dam/Worldbank/GEP/GEP2014b/ GEP2014b_EAP.pdf (Stand 02/09/2014)

WB (World Bank) (2014b): Global economic prospects. Latin America and the Caribbean, http://www.worldbank.org/content/dam/Worldbank/GEP/GEP2014b/ GEP2014b_LAC.pdf (Stand 02/09/2014)

Authors

Harald BERGBAUER

Dr. Harald Bergbauer is lecturer at the Bavarian School of Public Policy. He teaches political theory and political systems at this institution as well as at the University of Armed Forces Munich. He deals primarily with major political ideologies such as liberalism, conservatism, and socialism, as well as with the political systems of Germany, the European Union, and the United States of America. Currently he is working on a major study about liberalism and conservatism in post-war America. Recently he published studies on 20-century theoreticians like Eric Voegelin, Oswald Spengler, and Russell Kirk, current economic issues, international relations in the light of Samuel P. Huntington and Roger Scruton, et al. E-Mail: bergbauer@hfpm.de

Ralf GÖLLNER

Dr. Ralf Thomas Göllner is assistant professor at the University of Regensburg and visiting lecturer at the Bavarian School of Public Policy. He studied political sciences, history of Eastern Europe and economics at Ludwig-Maximilian-University in Munich, Germany, where he received his Ph.D. His main research and teaching are primarily on Central Eastern Europe's development after transition with foci on regional (cross-border) cooperation and integration, democratization and Europeanization, post-communist systems and elites as well as national and ethnic minorities in Europe. Recently he published studies on regional cooperation in Eastern Europe, minority and identity politics, and constitutional development in Eastern Europe.
E-Mail: ralf.goellner@ur.de

Werner GUMPEL

Prof. Gumpel occupied the Chair in South-East European Economics and Society and was President of Munich University's Institute of East and South-East European Economics until 1996. He has been a member of the teaching staff at the Bavarian School of Public Policy since 1965, and is Department Representative of Department III (Economics and Society). His main publications include: "Socialist Economic Systems" (1983), "German Unification and its Lessons for Korea" (co-ed., 1996), "Turkey as a Political and Economic Factor in Europe and Central Asia" (ed., 1999), and "The Relations of Turkey with Germany and the European Union" (ed., 2003). Prof. Gumpel is also editor of the series "Transformationsökonomie", of "Wirtschaft und Gesellschaft Südosteuropas", and co-editor of the journals "Osteuropa-Wirtschaft" and "Global Economic Review" (Seoul). (The English articles herein mentioned are published in German.). E-Mail: w.gumpel@t-online.de

Gottfried-Karl KINDERMANN

Dr. Dr. h. c. Gottfried-Karl Kindermann is professor em. and coordinator for International Politics at the Bavarian School of Public Policy, Chairman of the Interdisciplinary Committee for the History and Politics of East-and-Southeast Asia at the Ludwig Maximilian University of Munich, and Co-Chairman of the Foreign Affairs Association (Gesellschaft für Aussenpolitik). He developed a lasting interest in Korea when he served in 1950 as a student volunteer in the press section of the UN Security Council. Organizing two German-Korean conferences on divided nations, he started in 1975 and 1978 the Munich University's tradition of cooperation with Korean universities, a tradition that was actively renewed by Professor Werner Gumpel in 1985 in cooperation with the Korean Yonsei University. Professor Kindermann joined this endeavor from 1986 until the 12-th and last of those conferences in 1995. In 2005 Prof. Kindermann published in German a political history of Korea from the "Opening" of Korea until 2005 (Der Aufstieg Koreas in der Weltpolitik - The Rise of Korea in World Politics) that was prefaced by Korea's Ex-President Kim Dae Jung. E-Mail: fang_fang@hotmail.com

Sangtu KO

Dr. Sangtu Ko is a Professor at the Graduate School of Area Studies, Yonsei University. He has served as chair of the Research Committee (RC42), International Political Science Association and president of the Korean Association for Slavic Studies. His current research focuses on Russian foreign policy, middle power foreign policy and regional integration in Northeast Asia. His journal articles include "The Foreign Policy Goal of South Korea's UN Peacekeeping Operations," *International Peacekeeping*, 2015, "The Added Value of Partnership with NATO for South Korean Security," *Pacific Focus*, 2014, "The Causes of Fluctuating Anti-Americanism in South Korea," *The Korean Journal of Defense Analysis*, 2014 and "Korea's Middle Power Activism and Peacekeeping Operations," *Asia Europe Journal*, 2012. He edited a monograph *Risks and Opportunities of the Energy Sector in East Siberia and the Russian far East* (Münster: LIT Verlag, 2012). E-Mail: stko@yonsei.ac.kr

Doowon LEE

Doowon Lee is a Professor at the School of Economics, Yonsei University, Seoul, Korea. Currently he is the Director at the Institute of Continuing Education for the Future (ICEF) at Yonsei University. He has acquired his B.A. in business administration from Yonsei University in 1987 and his Ph.D. in economics from Northwestern University in 1991. Major careers include visiting professor at the University of California-San Diego (1992 and 2002), associate dean at the Graduate School of Economics in Yonsei University (2004-2008), associate dean at Underwood International College in Yonsei University (2007-2009), chair at School of Economics, Yonsei University (2010-2012), associate dean at Development Office of Yonsei University (2012-2014), visiting scholar at Columbia University (2009.9.-2010.8.), independent board member at the Korea Housing Finance Corporation (2008-2010) and KTB Investment & Securities (2013-2015), and general secretary at the Korean Economic Association (2011). He has published more than 60 academic papers, book chapters, and books. He joined domestic and international conferences more than 200 times. Also, he has contributed roughly 180 columns to domestic and international newspapers. In particular, he served as guest columnist to *Jungang Ilbo, Kungmin Ilbo, Munhwa Ilbo, and Donga Ilbo*. His area of interests lies in international economics, transition economics, and economics of development. In 2011, he was awarded *Market Economy Award: Media Contribution* by the Federation of Korean Industries. E-Mail: leedw104@yonsei.ac.kr

Taedong LEE

Taedong Lee is an associate professor at the Department of Political Science and International Relations in Yonsei University, Seoul. Lee has worked on sub-national environmental governance with perspectives of international relations and public policy. Lee recently (2014) published a monograph, "Global Cities and Climate Change: Translocal Relations of Environmental Governance" (Routledge), examining conditions entailed in cities' participation in international climate change networks, collaboration patterns in a global network, and variations in city-level climate change policies with multilevel modeling, social network analysis and case studies. His articles have appeared in journals including The Rise of International NGOs, Corruption and NGO sustainability (*Voluntas*), Media Independence and Trust in NGOs (*Nonprofit and Voluntary Sector Quarterly*), Building Green (*Review of Policy Research*), Global Cities and Transnational Climate Change Networks (*Global Environmental Politics*), Climate co-benefits (*Journal of Cleaner Production*), Policy Learning (*Policy Sciences*), Policy by Doing (Policy Studies Journal), Urban Mitigation Policy (Journal of Comparative Policy Analysis), Urban Energy Transition (Energy Policy) and Korea Citation Indexed journals. He is working on climate risk, adaptation policy and urban climate resilience to integrate disaster management and climate change policy. Topics of urban politics, village community making, and NGO politics are also his research interests. E-Mail: tdlee@yonsei.ac.kr

Rigmar OSTERKAMP

Rigmar Osterkamp is an economist who received his doctor degree (PhD) from Munich University. After some years as an assistant professor he joined the Ifo Institute for Economic Research, a Munich based German economic think tank where he became head of department for international economic policy comparisons. His specializations are on long-term economic growth, development policy, social policy and health economics. His recent publications comprise: *The Global Organ Shortage* (Stanford University Press, 2013; co-authored with R. Beard and D. Kaserman (Auburn University, U.S.); editor of: *Unconditional Basic Income for Germany?* (in German language, Nomos publishing house, 2015); several publications in internationally renowned journals. In 2007 he joined the University of Namibia for four years where he was Senior Lecturer for economics. Since many years he is lecturer for economics at Bavarian School of Public Policy, Munich.
E-Mail: rigmar.osterkamp@gmx.de

Heinz STEINMÜLLER

Prof. Dr. Heinz Steinmüller has retired from the Technical University of Munich and is at present a lecturer at the Bavarian School of Public Policy (HfP), Munich. He studied economics and sociology at the University of Munich and started his academic work as assistant professor at the University of Munich and at the University of Cologne. He did research work for the German Research Foundation at the London School of Economics and Political Science as well as the Centre for Environmental Studies, London. His preferred fields of research and academic teaching are: micro- and macroeconomics, urban economics and social policy. E-Mail: steinmueller@hfpm.de

Jona VAN LAAK

Jona van Laak is a valedictorian of the Bavarian School of Public Policy (HfP) and assistant of Prof. Dr. Heinz Steinmüller in the research project *The International Financial Crisis and its Effects for the World Economy*. He works as a tutor on the preparation of exams in the department of economics at the HfP. As a doctoral student of Prof. Dr. Wilhelm Hofmann he is researching on the theoretical dimensions of the state of emergency and their applications in crisis scenarios in the 21st century. E-Mail: jona@v-laak.de